Get Ready
Get Set
Go!

By Julee Roth

Photos by Gail S. Sleeman & others

jRc
Publications, Inc.
Post Office Box 6805
Snowmass Village
Colorado 81615

ISBN: 0-9637423-0-2

DEDICATION

Dedicating this book has been a difficult experience for me since so many people have been an influence and inspiration. Therefore, I would like to dedicate this book to the junior sailors at Great Lakes Yacht Club. They are an exceptional group that continue to inspire me to make sailing more fun and enjoyable.

I also want to dedicate this book to Avaram - my spirit through life - may your words of wisdom continue to echo.

Finally, I want to dedicate this book to all those willing to learn more. As in the words of Galileo, "You cannot teach a person anything. You can only help him find it for himself."

ACKNOWLEDGEMENTS

I am truly indebted to many people, without whose help and understanding you would not be holding this book. I am grateful that my parents sail and that I can still ask my Dad to crew for me. My Dad's devotion to sailing is second only to his devotion to his family.

To my friends: your support, encouragement and acceptance of my crazy endeavors keeps me floating on an even keel! No pun intended! Thank you Nancy, Sharon, Alicia, Eric, Randy, Lauren and Troy.

Special thanks to Tong and Suzanne for their efforts and suggestions during the first and final stages of this book. Lisa and Robin, thank you for your dedication, devotion and amazing artistic talents. Thank you Ryan—Ryan's Express saved me from the old hunt and peck. Last and certainly not least, thank you Carolyn for your invaluable editing skills.

I know that I will never be able to repay any of the kindness, generosity and tremendous effort that created this book and made my dreams a reality.

Thank you,

Julee

INTRODUCTION

GET READY GET SET GO! is an advanced sailing manual designed to further the knowledge of any basic sailor. You need not want to race to be an advanced sailor. However, I have made many references to racing since racing is a fun way to improve your skills. Be sure to use this book in conjunction with an accredited sailing course to benefit as much as possible.

Divided into three sections, most chapters begin with specific terms. All concepts are explained simply so sailors of all ages can understand and learn advanced sailing skills. Combined with many descriptions, illustrations and photographs, learning is fun and easy. At the end of the book is a self-test to check your knowledge.

Again, this book is designed to supplement your skills - contact the United States Sailing Association or the American Red Cross to find an instructional program in your area. Keep sailing safe and fun, learn more about our great sport! If you have any comments, questions or suggestions for future editions, please write to me at JRC Publications, Inc., Post Box 6805, Snowmass Village, CO 81615.

TABLE OF CONTENTS

TABLE OF CONTENTS

Steve Mundinger

1

TERMS

WIND

CLOUDS

WAVES

FORECAST

TERMS

AIR MASS A body of air that has the same pressure, temperature, and amount of moisture throughout the mass. Depending on its origination, an air mass can be stable or unstable, tropical (warm), polar (cold), continental (over land), or maritime (over water).

ANEMOMETER An instrument used to measure windspeed.

APPARENT WIND The direction and/or speed of the wind measured in a moving boat. Apparent wind appears to be coming from a direction more forward than the true wind, because it is a result of true wind plus the movement of the boat.

ATMOSPHERIC PRESSURE The weight of a column of air measured in either millibars or inches of mercury. This pressure rises and falls according to the altitude and temperature of air masses.

BAROMETER An instrument that measures atmospheric pressure.

CLOUDS The cooling of air produces water droplets that form into clouds.

FOG Low-level clouds that contain a lot of moisture. Fog occurs as warm air hits a cool surface.

FRONT The border between a warm air mass and a cool air mass.

1

HIGH PRESSURE	When cool, dry air sinks and barometric pressure increases.
HUMIDITY	The amount of water air can hold before becoming saturated.
JET STREAM	A "river" of air that circles the earth at 35,000 feet above sea level.
LIGHTNING	An electric charge.
LOW PRESSURE	When warm, moist air rises and barometric pressure decreases.
NAUTICAL MILE	A unit of measure used by travelers at sea and in the air. Distance is based on the curvature of the earth's surface. Also known as a knot.
PREVAILING WIND	The direction of the wind that predominates in a specific hemisphere.
RADIATION	The heating of the earth by the sun.
SQUALL	A fast-moving line of cold air that meets warm air. It usually results in a sudden thunderstorm that lasts between five and twenty minutes.

T E R M S

STATUTE MILE

A unit of measure based on a straight line of 5,280 feet. Primarily used in land distances and on newscasts, stated as miles per hour.

THUNDER

The sound caused by lightning when electricity heats the air suddenly.

TRUE WIND

The direction and/or speed of the wind when measured standing still.

VEER

A clockwise wind shift.

WAVE

The result of the wind as it hits the water.

WEATHER MAP

A map that shows the areas of high and low pressure, temperature differences and the probable direction that the weather will move.

WIND

The result of air flows moving from high pressure areas to low pressure areas.

WIND SHIFT

A change in direction of the wind that either backs (moves counter-clockwise) or veers (moves clockwise).

W I N D

1

Understanding the weather and the basic patterns that weather systems take will make any sailor much more knowledgeable. It is not surprising that some of the world's best sailors study past weather patterns to help predict their strategy and tactics for upcoming regattas.

HOW WE GET WIND

▲ The wind is a result of high-pressure areas moving toward low-pressure areas. **Atmospheric pressure**, **radiation** (heat), and **humidity** (moisture in the air) all combine to determine the direction and strength of the wind. If you know how these factors work together, you can make your own basic weather forecast.

A **front** is the border between air masses. A cold front of cool, dry air generally moves quickly towards an area of warm, moist air. When the air masses meet, a **squall** or **thunderstorm** may develop.

A warm front is just the opposite. This front moves slowly, lasts longer, and is not so stormy or violent — but any gray, rainy weather can last for days!

Weather map symbols for a warm front and cold front.

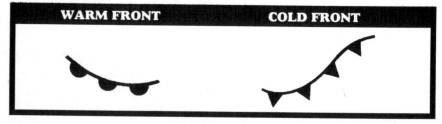

WHICH WAY?

▲ Wind is one of the most important ingredients in sailing. A racing sailor wants to know where on the course the wind will change direction or strength. Knowing which side is windiest and where wind shifts occur can make the difference between winning or losing the race. A cruising sailor needs to know where the wind will go to make navigational plans.

There is a general pattern to the wind that specifies which way the wind will go. The pictures below show the general directions of the wind for the Northern and Sothern Hemispheres.

Although the wind may move in one general direction, certain forces cause this direction to change. And it can change from one minute to the next!

Prevailing wind directions in each hemisphere.

The **jet stream**, which flows around the world like a river, is just one such force that influences wind direction. Located in the upper atmosphere, the stream weaves around the globe, pushing high and low pressure areas along.

WHAT IS ATMOSPHERIC PRESSURE?

▲ From the movement of high and low pressure areas, we measure the force of the air with a **barometer**. This force, or pressure, increases as well as decreases. A barometer is one of the best indicators of what the weather will do.

Wind in a **high pressure** area, or cell, tries to flow into a low pressure area. If you ever see a weather map with a big **H** over the region, this means a nice, sunny day, or days, for that region.

1

It is the low pressure cell that usually creates the most dramatic changes in the weather. A **low pressure** area can be smaller than a high pressure cell and can move a lot faster.

Also, the air in this low pressure cell moves up, causing the air to cool and condense into moisture.

The more condensation, the heavier the rain, and the longer the bad weather. The closer the high and low pressure areas are to each other, the greater the difference of atmospheric pressure, and the stronger the wind in the region.

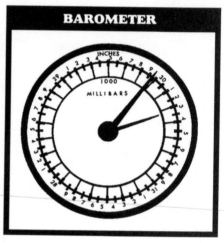

BAROMETER

HOW DO WE MEASURE THE WIND?

▲The strength of the wind is measured with an **anemometer** and is indicated in **knots** or nautical miles per hour. This is different from measuring in **statute** miles per hour, the way most weather forecasters give their reports.

Sailors use two types of measurements to determine the wind's strength and direction. Measuring the wind while standing still is called a **true measurement.** When you are out sailing and you make a wind calculation, you are making an **apparent measurement.**

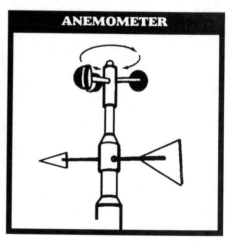

ANEMOMETER

If the wind is measured while the boat is moving, the wind appears stronger and seems to be coming from a new direction. The faster an object moves, the further forward the wind feels like it is moving.

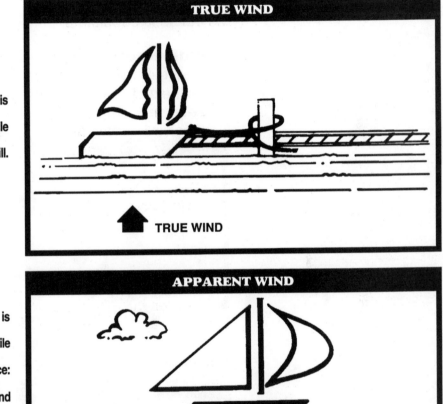

True wind is measured while standing still.

Apparent wind is measured while moving. Notice: the apparent wind seems to be coming from a new direction.

1

SOME LIKE IT HOT!

▲ When the sun heats the Earth — this is called **radiation** — the difference between the hotter and cooler areas creates wind. A **sea breeze** is a great example of the sun creating wind by heating the land. As the hot air rises off the land, it is pulled into a cool air region, such as over the ocean. Then the wind builds in strength and heads from the water back to the shore. Because the Earth rotates, the wind may **veer** about 10 degrees per hour before the sun sets. The wind can shift as much as 60 degrees during the day.

A **land breeze** is just the opposite and usually occurs at night when the land is cooler than the water. A land breeze is sometimes called an offshore breeze, while a sea breeze is an onshore breeze.

HOLY HURRICANES!

▲ Hurricanes and typhoons (as they are called in the Pacific Ocean) are seasonal storms that begin as small tropical storms. They move slowly across warm equatorial waters, picking up moisture and building in intensity. As these storms move away from the equator, they become giant whirlwinds of air, spiraling around a low pressure cell. See the Safir/Simpson scale for the categories of wind speeds.

WHY HURRICANES ARE DEADLY

▲ Although hurricane winds can be clocked at over 200 miles per hour, and whole communities can be wiped out, it is not the winds that do the most amount of damage.

Being prepared for a disaster saves lives and prevents damage.

The number one cause of death and destruction is flooding. Before the hurricane hits land, a storm surge of water, sometimes 20-30 feet above sea level, comes ashore, wiping out bridges, highways, and even buildings. Then, during the actual storm, torrential rains continue to flood the area.

Just when everything appears to be dying down, the eye, or center, of the hurricane passes, bringing the next half of the storm.

1

AND AFTER...

▲ Hurricanes die quickly once they are over land because the storms need the warm, open water to survive. And although hurricanes are becoming easier to predict, the National Oceanic and Atmospheric Administration (NOAA) still has a difficult time knowing exactly where a storm will hit and with what force. NOAA and the National Hurricane Center in Florida use satellites, radar, Air Force planes and other tools to aid their predictions.

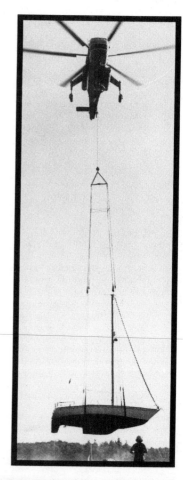

SAFIR/SIMPSON CHART				
Category	Winds Between	Storm Surge	Barometric Pressure	Damage
1	74-95 MPH	4-5 Ft	28.94	No real damage to buildings, some coastal flooding.
2	96-110 MPH	6-8 Ft	28.50-28.93	Moderate damage to buildings, considerable damage to vegetation, and flooding is probable.
3	111-130 MPH	9-12 Ft	27.91-28.49	Extensive damage and flooding is possible up to six miles inshore.
4	131-155 MPH	13-18 Ft	27.17-27.90	Major beach erosion, major structural damage, and considerable flooding.
5	over 155 MPH	over 18 Ft	< 27.17	Damage is catastrophic, flooding may occur 5-10 miles inshore.

THE BEAUFORT SCALE

▲ British Admiral Sir Francis Beaufort divided the force of the wind into thirteen categories, 0-12, in 1805. Maritime weather forecasters still give forecasts in his system. See if you can find one on a VHF radio tuned to the national weather (listen for the "mafor" broadcast).

BEAUFORT CHART		
Beaufort Number	**Wind Speed**	**What to look for**
0	0-1	Mirror-like water. No waves.
1	1-3	Little ripples on the water. No waves.
2	4-6	Large ripples. Waves 0-1/3 foot.
3	7-10	Some waves, top of wave may break off. Waves 1-3 feet.
4	11-16	White caps form on top of the waves. Waves 3-5 feet.
5	17-21	Pronounced waves, some spray. Waves 5-7 feet.
6	22-27	Large waves, white caps and definite spray. Waves 7-9 feet.
7	28-33	Moderate gale, white foam streaks on water. Waves 9-11 feet.
8	34-40	Gale force, white foam in direction of wind. Waves 11-14 feet.
9	41-47	Heavy spray where the top of wave breaks off. Waves 14-20 feet.
10	48-55	Stormy, no visibility from blowing spray. Waves 20-30 feet.
11	56-63	Very violent seas. Waves and large swells.
12	over 64	Hurricane strength, no visibility. Waves over 30 feet.

WIND

WINDS AROUND THE WORLD		
Name	**Type of Storm**	**Where Found**
Baguio	Tropical Storm	Phillipines
Blizzard	Snowstorm	North America
Bora	Cold Mountain Wind	Adriatic
Chinook	Warm Mountain Wind	Rocky Mtns.
Cordonazo	Tropical Storm	Central America
Cyclone	Tropical Storm	Indian Ocean
Etesian	Summer Wind	Aegean
Fallvaer	Violent Mountain Squall	Norway
Fohn	Warm Mountain Wind	European Alps
Gale	Extremely Strong Wind	Worldwide
Gregale	Moist NE Wind	Southern Italy
Harmatten	Dry Trade Wind	Guinea Coast
Hurricane	Violent Tropical Storm	Caribbean
Khamsin	Hot Desert Wind	Egypt
Meltemi	Strong North Wind	Greece
Mistral	Cold Mountain Wind	Southern France
Monsoon	Biannual Land/Sea Wind	Indian Ocean
Northerly	Polar Gale	North America

W I N D

WINDS AROUND THE WORLD		
Name	**Type of Storm**	**Where Found**
Norwester	Mountain Wind	New Zealand
Pampero	Gale of South Polar Wind	South America
Santa Ana	Mountain Wind	California
Simoom	Sandstorm	North Africa
Sirocco	Wet or Dry Wind	Mediterranean
Sumatra	Mountain Wind	Malacca
S. Sea Hurricane	Tropical Storm	South Pacific
Southerly Buster	Gale of South Polar Wind	South Pacific
Squall	Fast Moving Storm	Worldwide
Typhoon	Violent Tropical Storm	North Pacific
Tornado	Whirlwind	North Pacific
Trade Wind	Steady NE or SE Wind	30 N to 30 S Lat.
Tramontana	Cold North Wind	W. Mediterranean
Thunderstorm	Slower Moving Storm	Worldwide
Waterspout	Violent Wind Over Water	All Oceans
Williwaw	Violent Mountain Wind	Argentina/Chile
Willy-Willy	Tropical Storm	South Pacific
Zonda	Mountain Wind	Argentina

CLOUDS

1 NOT JUST ANOTHER CLOUDY DAY....

▲ **Clouds** come in three basic forms and are found at three different levels of the atmosphere. The high-altitude clouds (from 1,600 to 45,000 feet above sea level) are cirrus, cirrocumulus, and cirrostratus. They are usually big and fluffy like cotton balls.

The middle altitude clouds (from 6,500 to 23,000 feet) are altocumulus, altostratus, and nimbostratus. These look thin and gray, indicating rain in the near future.

And finally, there are the low-altitude clouds (from the ground to 7,000 feet). Stratocumulus are sometimes white and can cover the entire sky; stratus clouds are foggy and gray. Cumulus at this low level can build into thunderstorms; cumulonimbus are thunderclouds. It is the middle- and lower-level clouds that sailors need to be concerned with because they warn of impending weather changes.

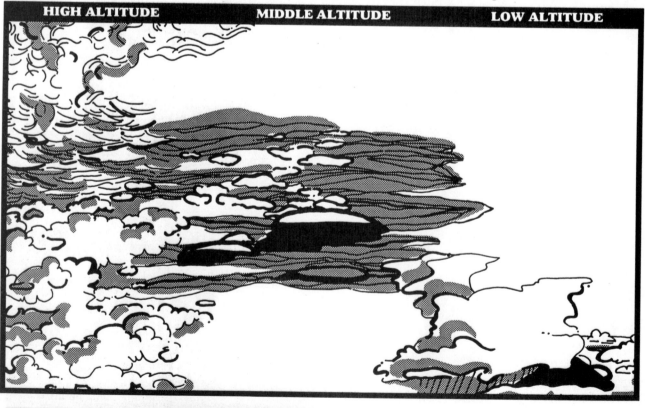

HIGH ALTITUDE   MIDDLE ALTITUDE   LOW ALTITUDE

As a rule, sailors sail towards the clouds, since the pressure and temperature changes associated with clouds can mean more wind. Sometimes there may be more wind in the area around the cloud than directly under the cloud.

IT'S FROGGY OUT!

▲ **Fog** usually creeps up anytime when cool air hits a warm, moist area. A few types of fog are:
- Mist or steam fog
- Smog
- Radiation fog
- Advection fog
- Adiabatic fog

Mist or steam fog is air that moves over a body of warm water. You can create this type of fog if you turn on the hot water in your cold bathroom. Any mirror or window pane would show how much moisture is in the air. Smog is simply a combination of fog and smoke. Radiation fog is the kind found at night. After a warm, humid day, the calm, clear night sky is cooler than the land; moisture over the land cools, producing this fog. Advection fog is usually found at sea. This is a warm body of air moving over a cool body of water. Finally, adiabatic fog forms when the air expands and cools over a warm surface. Generally, this type of fog occurs as air moves up a mountain slope.

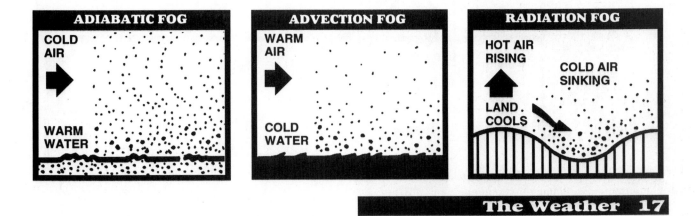

ADIABATIC FOG

COLD AIR

WARM WATER

ADVECTION FOG

WARM AIR

COLD WATER

RADIATION FOG

HOT AIR RISING

COLD AIR SINKING

LAND COOLS

1

THE NEW WAVE

▲ **Waves** are caused as wind hits the water. The size of waves depends on how strong the wind is, how deep the water is, how large the body of water is and how long the wind has been blowing.

Swells are waves from a distant storm. Because the storm was far away and because a wave can travel hundreds or thousands of miles, a swell is simply a wave losing its height.

Waves are measured from the top, or crest, to the bottom, or trough. The windier the day, the larger the wave and the further the wave will travel.

WHAT HAPPENS WHEN...

▲ There are many charts available from the National Weather Service or the National Oceanic and Atmospheric Administration to help you predict the weather in your area. Using the

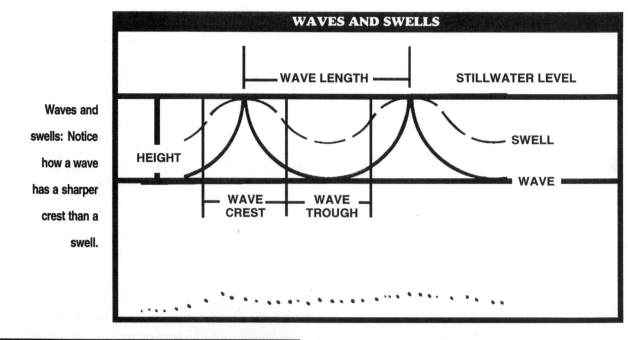

Waves and swells: Notice how a wave has a sharper crest than a swell.

WAVES AND SWELLS

WAVE LENGTH · STILLWATER LEVEL

SWELL

HEIGHT

WAVE

WAVE CREST · WAVE TROUGH

Beaufort scale, knowing cloud patterns, and listening to the weather forecasts will help you determine sailing conditions. You will have a better idea of which sails to use, which side of a race course is favored, or what preparations to make for incoming weather.

A forecast based on the MAFOR scale (below) can be a precise tool in determining the weather, especially when combined with a barometric pressure reading.

Some points to remember:
- When temperatures decrease and barometric pressure decreases slowly, bad weather is approaching.
- When temperatures increase and barometric pressure increases slowly, good weather is approaching.
- Any time the pressure falls fast, expect a squall or thunder-storm.

MAFOR CHART

DECODE FOR LAKE AND SEAWAY MARINE FORECASTS

MAFOR $YYG_1 G_1/$ (NAME OF LAKE) 1 GDF_mW_1

KEYWORD (Indicating Marine Forecast)	DAY OF MONTH (GMT)	TIME(GMT) FORECAST PERIOD BEGINS	SOLIDUS	NAME OF LAKE OR SEAWAY*	GROUP INDICATOR	FORECAST PERIOD	WIND DIRECTION	WIND SPEED	FORECAST WEATHER	SIGNIFICANT WAVE HEIGHTS IN FEET AT END OF MESSAGE FOR EACH LAKE
	YY	G_1G_1				G	D	F_m	W_1	
MAFOR	06	12	(/)	SUPERIOR*	1	8	P	3	0	WAVES 5 TO 10 FEET

G - FORECAST PERIOD

0 - Conditions at beginning of forecast period
1 - Valid for 3 hours
2 - Valid for 6 hours
3 - Valid for 9 hours
4 - Valid for 12 hours
5 - Valid for 18 hours
6 - Valid for 24 hours
7 - Valid for 48 hours
8 - Valid for 72 hours
9 - Occasionally

D-WIND DIRECTION

0 - Calm
1 - Northeast
2 - East
3 - Southeast
4 - South
5 - Southwest
6 - West
7 - Northwest
8 - North
9 - Variable

F_m-WIND SPEED

0 - 0 to 10 knots
1 - 11 to 16 knots
2 - 17 to 21 knots
3 - 22 to 27 knots
4 - 28 to 33 knots
5 - 34 to 40 knots
6 - 41 to 47 knots
7 - 48 to 55 knots
8 - 56 to 63 knots
9 - 64 knots & above

W_1 - FORECAST WEATHER

0 - Moderate or good visibility, more than 3 nautical miles
1 - Risk of accumulation of ice on super-structures (Temp. 23° to 32° F.)
2 - Strong risk, accumulation of ice on superstructures (Temp. below 23°F.)
3 - Mist (visibility 5/8 to 3 nautical miles)
4 - Fog (visibility less than 5/8 nautical miles)
5 - Drizzle
6 - Rain
7 - Snow, or rain and snow
8 - Squally weather with or without showers
9 - Thunderstorms

*Statement in plain language of Gale or Storm warnings, if any, will follow name of lake or seaway. Times in Eastern Standard Time (EST). (Small Craft Advisories are not included in MAFOR Broadcasts).

The forecast 1GDF_mW_1 may be repeated as many times as necessary to describe the changes in wind and weather expected in a given area during the 24-hour forecast period. The forecast 1GDF_mW_1 in which G=1-8, refers to the forecast weather commencing at the time given in the group $YYG_1G_1/$ and continuing through the period indicated by G. Subsequent 1 GDF_mW_1 (G=1-8) indicate the period of time that the described weather is forecast to persist, commencing at the end of the period specified in the preceding group 1GDF_mW_1 (G=1-8). Any forecast 1GDF_mW_1 (G=1-8) may be followed by 1GDF_mW_1 (G=9); in such cases, G=9 indicates a phenomenon forecast to occur occasionally in the forecast period. On occasion, plain language words are used to describe weather conditions not easily described by the code tables; times are stated in EST.

Wave forecast indicates the expected wave heights at the downwind end or side of the lake; this being the area where the wave height buildup is greatest. Times in EST. Wave heights are usually specified as a range for the 24-hour period, but significant changes (generally variations of more than 5 feet) will be stated.

Note: Forecast periods begin at 0000, 0600, 1200, and 1800 Greenwich Mean Time; the equivalent Eastern Standard Times are 7 pm, 1 am, 7 am, and 1 pm.

TERMS
TIDES
CURRENTS
WATER FLOW

T E R M S

CURRENT	The horizontal, or sideways, flow of water.
DIURNAL	One high tide and one low tide per day.
EBB CURRENT	An outward flow of the water.
FLOOD CURRENT	An inward flow of the water.
HIGH TIDE	When the flood current brings the water in and the water is at the highest level.
LEEWAY	The sideways movement of the boat due to a tide or current.
LOW TIDE	When the ebb current takes the water out and the water level is at its lowest.
NEAP TIDE	The smallest difference in tidal range that occurs during the first quarter and last quarter of the moon phases.
SEMI-DIURNAL	Two high tides per day and two low tides per day.
SLACK TIDE	The time in between tides when there is no current.
SPRING TIDE	The highest of high tides or the lowest of low tides that occurs during the new and full moon phases.
TIDAL RANGE	The difference between high and low tides.
TIDE	The vertical, or up and down, water flow from the gravitational pull between the Earth and the moon.
TIDE TABLES	The table that predicts when the high, low or slack tides will occur each day.

T I D E S

2

ISN'T TIDE A DETERGENT?

▲ A **tide** is the movement of water vertically (up and down). Tides can also move horizontally (across) as they come to shore or move away from shore — this is a tidal current.

Tides are caused by the gravitational pull between the earth and the moon. This pull allows one-half of the earth to experience a high tide while the other half experiences a low tide.

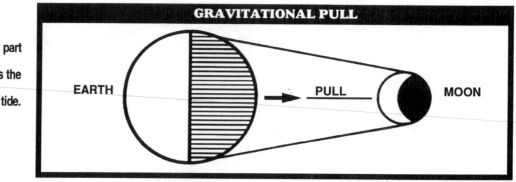

The shaded part on the Earth is the area with high tide.

Tides are smallest when the moon is in its first or last quarter, because that's when it exerts the least pull. When the moon is full or is a new moon, tides rise and fall the most.

The National Oceanic and Atmospheric Administration (NOAA) produces **tide tables** that should always be checked before sailing. In some areas of the United States, water levels can change from a few inches to as much as forty feet with each tide change. Interestingly enough, because lakes such as the Great Lakes are not large enough bodies of water, they don't experience tides.

Check the tide table before sailing to ensure a safe passage.

TIDE TABLE				
Date	8/12	8/13	8/14	8/15
High	10:03	10:51	11:41	12:31
Low	16:00	16:47	17:34	18:23
Slack	13:00	13:50	14:39	15:24

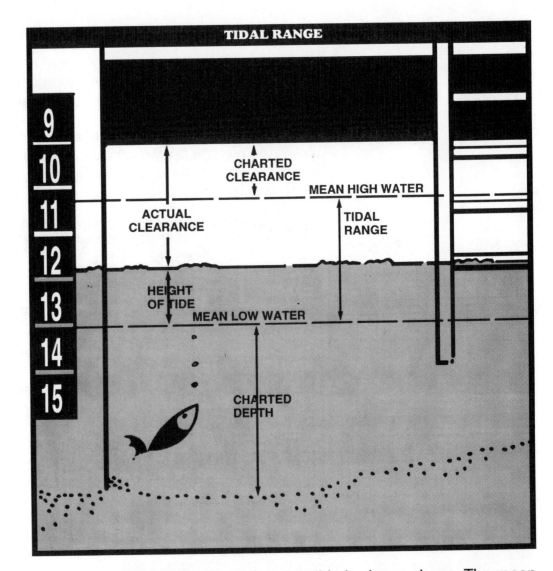

The height of a high or low tide is shown above. The mean high water is the average height of the high tide while the mean low water is the opposite. The **tidal range** is the difference between the two tides. Charted clearance, actual clearance and charted depth are used to determine if boats can clear a bridge or other obstruction.

IT'S A CURRENT AFFAIR

▲ A **current** is the horizontal movement of water. When one body of water is higher than another, a current results. For example, Lake Michigan is higher than Lake Huron; where Michigan flows into Huron, the current is strong. The speed of a current is measured in knots per hour. The deeper the water and the smaller the width, the faster the current. The reverse is also true — the shallower the water and the greater the width, the slower the current.

A current or tide can push you away from a mark. Think about what might happen if it came from the other direction.

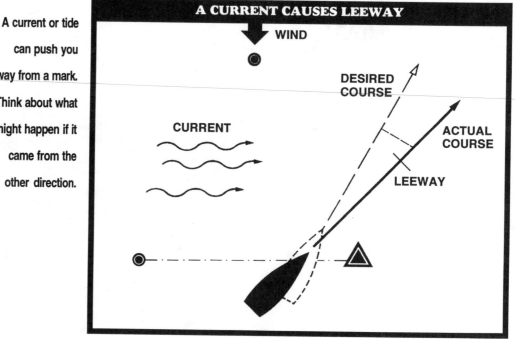

A CURRENT CAUSES LEEWAY

WIND

DESIRED COURSE

CURRENT

ACTUAL COURSE

LEEWAY

Another type of current occurs in a river — going upriver means going against the current, downriver means going with the current. The speed of the current or river flow is also measured in knots per hour.

The last type of current occurs when the wind blows in one direction for more than twelve hours. The direction of this current is at a forty-five degree angle to the direction that the wind blows.

WATER FLOW

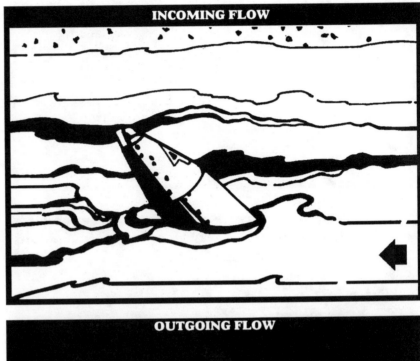

INCOMING FLOW

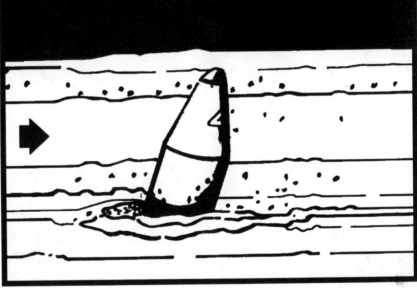

OUTGOING FLOW

Tides and currents both move the water, as seen in these two illustrations. The **flood current** (or tide) pushes the buoy as the water comes into shore. Hours later, the **ebb current** (or tide) shows the water moving out.

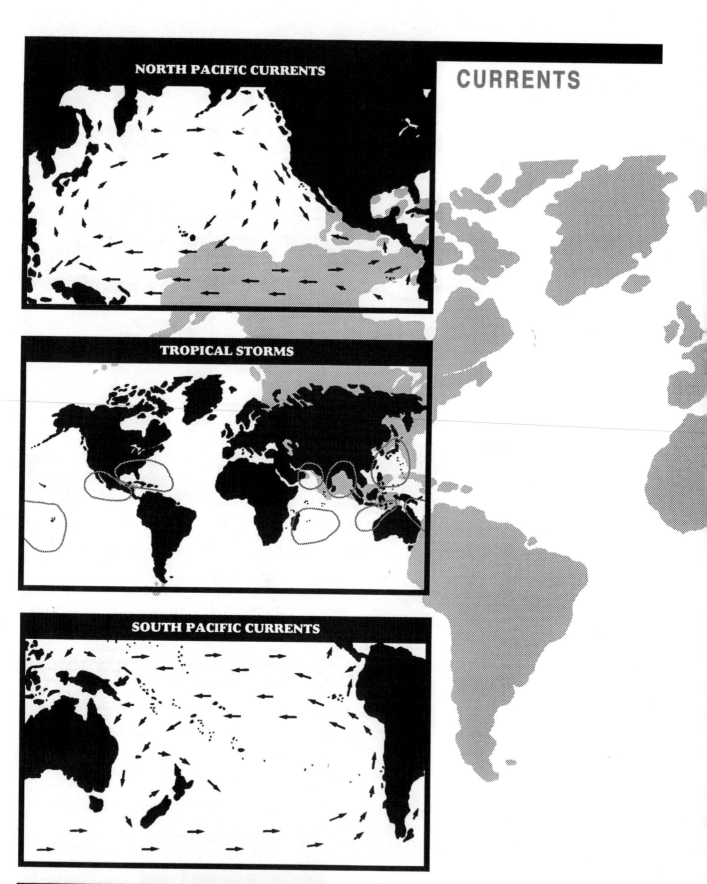

NORTH PACIFIC CURRENTS

CURRENTS

TROPICAL STORMS

SOUTH PACIFIC CURRENTS

NORTH ATLANTIC CURRENTS

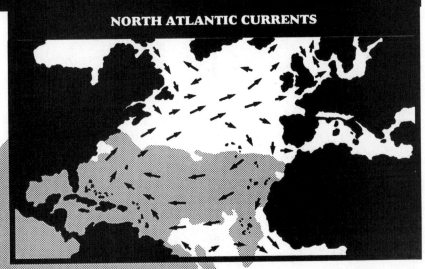

INDIAN OCEAN CURRENTS

SOUTH ATLANTIC CURRENTS

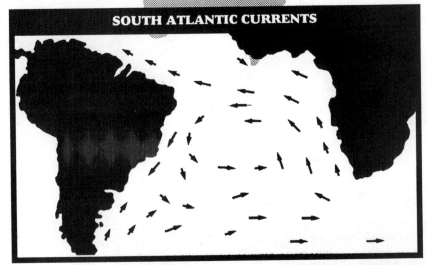

3

TERMS   **LIFT**
FORCE   **DRAG**
FLUIDS   **FRICTION**

T E R M S

AERODYNAMICS The physical force of the air.

AIRFOIL A foil designed to create lift when air flow hits it.

CENTER OF EFFORT (CE) A point on a sail where aerodynamic forces meet to create lift.

CENTER OF LATERAL RESISTANCE (CLR) A point on the centerboard or keel where hydrodynamic forces meet to help lift the boat.

CONCAVE An inward curve.

CONVEX An outward curve.

DISTURBED AIR OR WATER The term for wind or water that has not rejoined the free-flowing air or water stream.

DRAG A force that resists the motion of an object.

FOIL The shape of certain objects, designed to produce the most lift and the least drag.

FORCE Pressure against an object resulting in a push or pull.

FORCE VECTOR A line showing the direction the force is going.

FORM FRICTION Friction that occurs when airfoils or hydrofoils are not designed properly.

FRICTION Resistance against an object.

T E R M S

3

HEEL

When the force of the wind or water acts on a boat, causing it to angle or incline.

HYDROFOIL

A foil designed to create lift in the water.

HYDRODYNAMICS

The physical force of the water.

KNOCK

A change in the boat's course when the wind shifts, causing the boat to go away from the new wind.

LIFT

There are two types of lift. One is a change in the boat's course when the wind shifts, causing the boat to head toward the new wind (also known as veer). Another type of lift results from the high and low air pressures acting on an object, causing it to move.

RESULTANT FORCE

The total force created when lift and drag are combined.

STAGNATION POINT

A point where velocity, or speed, is zero.

STALLING

The point on the foil where the airflow or waterflow is too disturbed, keeping the foil from working properly.

SKIN FRICTION

Friction that occurs under water and is due to items like a dirty boat bottom, poor paint job, or too large a propeller.

SAILS MAKE THE BOAT GO

▲ By now, you know that the true engine of a sailboat is the sail. Just by trimming the sail in or letting the sail out, you can make the boat head in a particular direction. But, by changing the centerboard height, vang tension, the amount of outhaul or any other sail control, you can change the boat's **hydrodynamic** and/or **aerodynamic** shapes. This may sound too scientific or confusing, but the principles of what makes a boat move are quick and easy to learn.

MAY THE FORCE BE WITH YOU

▲ A **force** pushes or pulls on an object, creating pressure. Draw a line with an arrow at one end and you've drawn a **force vector**; it shows the direction in which the force is applied.

Two types of forces concern sailors: lift and drag. When a boat moves through the water at a constant speed, the force of the air (**CE**) on the sails and the force of the water (**CLR**) on the centerboard or keel create a resultant force. The resultant force powers the boat.

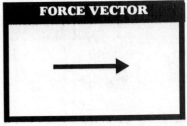

FORCE VECTOR

FLUIDS

FIVE FLUID FACTS

▲ Sir Isaac Newton, Professor Daniel Bernoulli, and G. B. Venturi each discovered certain principles that make sail theory a little easier to understand.

1. The wind and water are both fluids and act the same.
2. Free-flowing air streams in straight, parallel lines. Free-flowing air is also attracted to low pressure areas and is repelled by high-pressure areas. Free-flowing air resists change and thus sticks to the convex side of an object.
3. When free-flowing air travels under 126 miles per hour, the air is compressible, which means it can be compacted.
4. Air velocity (speed) increases when air passes through restricted zones or narrow passageways.
5. When the velocity of an object increases, the surrounding air pressure drops.

Wind and water behave the same; they go around whatever is in their way.

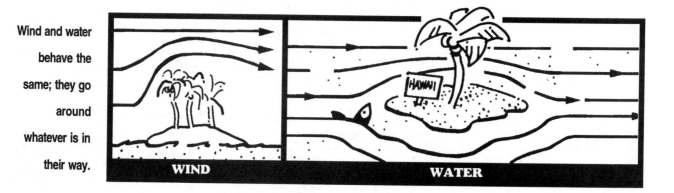

WIND

WATER

Together, these five fluid facts scientifically prove Newton's finding that for every action, there is an equal and opposite reaction. This means that whatever happens to the sails has an equal yet opposite effect on the centerboard/keel. So if a gust of wind hits the sails, the boat would **heel** to leeward, while the centerboard/keel would rise to windward. Bernoulli discovered that for any fluid, like air, an increase in velocity results in a drop in air pressure, so long as the air is traveling under 126 miles per hour. The opposite is also true: a decrease in speed results in an increase in air pressure. This means that as the wind hits the sails, the wind divides around the sail, with the wind pushing harder around the **convex** part.

Venturi came up with the concept of an infinite number of "tubes" in the air stream. When an air tube is forced around the curved part of an object, the air compresses and accelerates to quickly rejoin the free-flowing air, again, so long as the air is traveling under 126 miles per hour.

Combined, Newton, Bernoulli and Venturi discovered the Theory of Lift — the principles behind what makes a sailboat go or even what makes an airplane rise into the air.

HUH?

▲ As the air flows around the sail, the air flow separates, causing the sail to have high pressure on one side and a counteracting low pressure on the other side. The **stagnation point**, found on the forward, leading edge of the **foil**, is where the air velocity is zero and the amount of air pressure is the greatest. On either side of the stagnation point, where the air separates on the sail, the **disturbed** air flow accelerates to

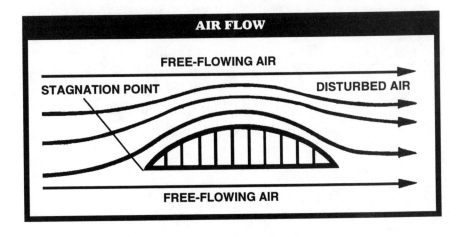

AIR FLOW

FREE-FLOWING AIR

STAGNATION POINT

DISTURBED AIR

FREE-FLOWING AIR

rejoin the free flowing air. This "flattens" the edge of the foil and the high pressure area is drawn to the low pressure area, making the boat lift, or sail in a certain direction. This lift, while horizontal, is the same as the vertical lift of an airplane.

As free-flowing air hits the foil, it separates and quickly rejoins the air flow, moving the boat forward.

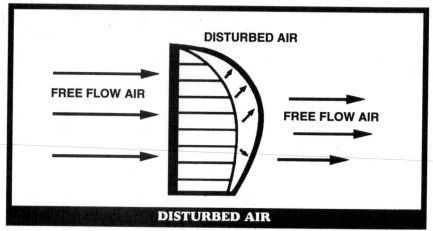

LIFT ME UP!

▲ Sailors experience two types of **lift**. The first type was explained above; the second type happens when the wind shifts. They both have common themes:

- Lift is the force that counteracts gravity.
- Lift is caused by the motion of air and water on an object.
- Lift is the result of the principles of fluid flows.
- Lift acts at a 90-degree angle to drag.
- Lift results from the Center of Effort and the Center of Lateral Resistance working together.

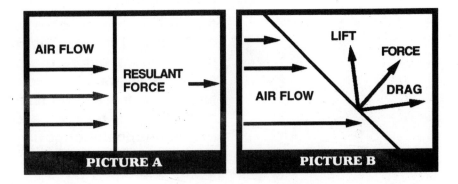

See what happens to lift in the following illustrations. In picture A, air pushes an object in the direction of the force. In picture B, as the angle of the object is changed, it produces three effects: lift, force, and drag.

WHAT A DRAG!

▲ **Drag** is the force that opposes lift. Usually drag flows in the direction of the wind. But drag can also result from a tidal stream, a current, or anything that resists the lifting force. When drag is combined with lift, the **resultant force** determines the direction the boat will go.

The average of lift and drag equals the force, determining the new direction of the object.

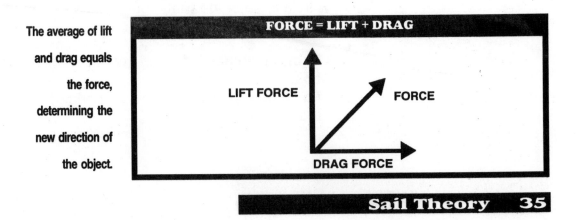

FRICTION

3

THE FLUID BENEATH THE BOAT

▲ As the forces of lift and drag react against the sails, the water flowing beneath the boat behaves in the same way as the air. This is because the hull, centerboard/keel, and rudder are **hydrofoil** shapes. The sails are called **airfoils**, and both hydrofoils and airfoils are designed as convex shapes to maximize lift and minimize drag. This means that an overturned rudder or an overtrimmed sail would create more drag than lift. This resistance causes **friction** and **stalling**, keeping the boat from moving efficiently through the water. As a consequence, you cannot travel as fast as possible.

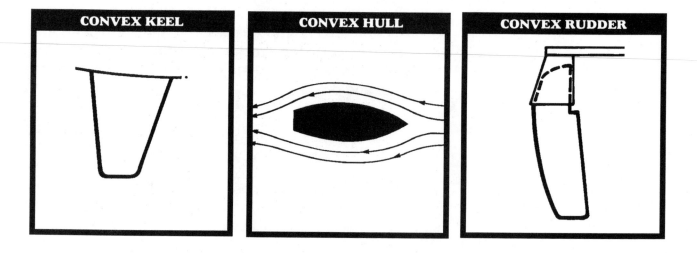

| CONVEX KEEL | CONVEX HULL | CONVEX RUDDER |

RESIST!

▲ The force of the wind counteracts friction the most. On a boat, friction comes in many forms.

- **Skin resistance** is friction from the underwater parts of the boat.
- **Form resistance** is friction that originates in the design of the airfoils or hydrofoils.

FRICTION

This boat is sailing smoothly because it has very little friction.

- Large waves, too much heeling, or too much leeway can all cause friction.
- A poorly designed mast and/or rigging can create too much friction aloft.

Friction can easily be reduced by simple adjustments or changes, thus allowing you to sail faster and better. The idea is to eliminate any air or water brakes on the boat. The most efficient way to sail is to allow the air and water to flow freely around the boat.

4

TERMS   **RIGGING**
TUNING   **WEATHER HELM**
BALANCE   **REDUCING HEEL**

T E R M S

BABY STAY — A wire that supports the aft pull of the mast.

BACKSTAY — A wire that supports the forward pull of the mast.

CENTER LINE — An imaginary line drawn down the middle of the boat from the bow to stern.

CENTER OF EFFORT — The exact position of the force of the wind on the sails.

CENTER OF LATERAL RESISTANCE — The location of the counter-acting force to center of effort found in an exact location on the centerboard or keel.

CHAINPLATES — Metal plates affixed to the hull that help take the weight or pressure load off the shrouds.

DRAFT — The center of curve on a sail.

ENTRY — The curve of the leading edge of the sail. (The leading edge is the part that hits the wind first.)

EXIT — The leech area, where the wind leaves the sail.

FALLING OFF — Going away from the wind.

FULLNESS — The depth, belly, or sag in the sail.

LEE HELM — What happens when the boat points away from the wind when you let go of the helm.

LIFT — Heading up into the wind.

MAST RAKE — The amount of tension of the backstay with the sails raised.

NEUTRAL HELM — When the boat continues straight when you let go of the helm.

T E R M S

4

PRE-BEND   When the mast is bent backwards without the sails raised.

RIG   The mast and fittings used to hold the mast up.

RIGGING   Preparing the boat to sail and/or preparing the mast and shrouds to sail.

RIG TENSION   The amount of pressure on the shrouds.

RUNNING/BACK STAYS   Control the head stay tension.

RUNNING RIGGING   Rigging used for sail controls such as halyards and sheets.

SHROUD (SIDESTAY)   The side guide wires holding up the mast.

SPREADERS   Struts (metal pieces) attached to the mast to keep the mast from bending improperly from the pushing or pulling of the shroud.

STANDING RIGGING   The mast's permanent fixtures like shrouds, spreaders and turn buckles.

TELLTALES   Yarn or strings attached to the sail that show airflow.

TUNING   Fine adjustments made to the mast and sails to achieve a well-balanced boat, thus making it sail better.

TURNBUCKLES   A fitting that allows the shroud to be attached to the boat with opposite threads on each piece so that they can be tightened without turning the shroud.

TWIST   The change in the leech angle of the main sail to the wind when looking from the bottom up.

WEATHER HELM   When the boat points into the wind when you let go of the tiller or wheel.

IF I CAN TUNE A BOAT, HOW COME I CAN'T TUNA FISH?

▲ To get the most from your boat, you need to be sure it is tuned properly. This means that there must be a balance between the **Center of Effort (CE)** and the **Center of Lateral Resistance (CLR)**. The force of the wind on the sails must be equal to the weight of the boat and crew to keep the boat upright and sailing well, or "on her lines."

In the pictures below, three lines are drawn from the corners of a flat sail. Where they meet is considered the CE. When you move the draft of the sail with any combination of the halyard, outhaul, vang, backstay, mainsheet or cunningham, the CE moves.

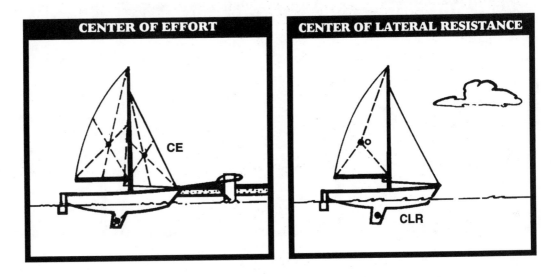

WHERE'S THE CLR?

▲ The CLR is the point that has an equal yet opposite effect on the force of the wind. Usually located on the centerboard or keel, the CLR changes positions with the crew and weight placement. Raising the centerboard, letting the sail out, or trimming in the sail also move the CLR.

THE PERFECTLY BALANCED BOAT

▲ When the CE and CLR are equal and aligned, the boat will sail upwind in a straight line. This is called having **neutral helm**. If the boat points into the wind as the helm is let go, this is **weather helm**. **Lee helm** is just the opposite, when the boat sails away from the wind as the helm is let go.

As a skipper, you always want some weather helm. This is because you always need hydrodynamic lift from the rudder. The feel of the helm should be comfortable, not hard to turn, and always in a "driving" mode. Weather helm increases **lift** and reduces **leeway** or sailing sideways. Before continuing on about weather helm, let's look at the rig.

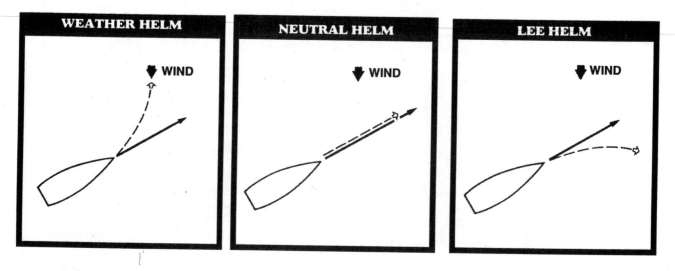

TUNING THE RIG

▲ The **standing rigging** — mast, spreaders, and shrouds — must be adjusted for many reasons. The most important reason, as mentioned above, is to balance the boat so that sailing on a port tack will produce the same results as sailing on a starboard tack.

FIRST THINGS FIRST

▲ After the mast has been stepped, or put up, attach all shrouds. Remember that the mast base must be secure in the mast step. Use a tape measure with the main halyard to check the length of each sidestay. Make each sidestay equal by either tightening or easing the turnbuckles on each side of the boat. Remember to keep minimal tension on the fore and backstays. One good way to adjust a stay is to take two to four turns on one side, measure, and adjust the other side by two to four turns of the turnbuckle. Remember that wire stays stretch and they may need adjusting each time you sail.

Olympic sailors check their tuning & rigging

Stock Newport/Onne Van Der Wal

Stock Newport/Daniel Forster

When looking up the mast, there should be no "S" curves or bends to one side of the mast. Again, measure the shrouds; they should be at equal measurements when the mast is perfectly tuned. If you find an "S" or a bend, and you are not quite sure what to do, pull on the shrouds while looking up the mast. If pulling on one fixes the "S," then tighten that shroud. Look up, or sight, the mast again.

Next, give your mast some pre-bend or mast rake before you raise the mainsail. You can do this by:

▲ Putting wooden blocks behind the mast at deck level (assuming your mast goes through the deck)

▲ Angle your spreaders aft (this also creates lift!)

▲ Tension the lower shrouds equally

Checking the

mast.

Most championship sailors take a tension gauge, vise grips or other tools out on the water to have perfect tuning for specific conditions. The boat manufacturer or your sail maker may have a tuning guide designed for your type of sails and boat.

Finally, check your spreaders. When properly set up, the spreaders can help create lift, reduce drag, and take up tension from the shrouds.

ARE WE IN TUNE YET?

▲ Once you have basically tuned the rig, go out for a sail. What does the boat feel like? Are you having problems steering upwind? Sight up the mast, looking from the bow to the stern. Any "S" curves? Does the mast lean to one side? Tack, look up the mast again. Any differences?

If the mast "falls off," or bends to the leeward side, ease the "straight" side and tighten the loose side until the mast appears straight. Sometimes the reason for this "falling off" to leeward is the unequal length of the spreaders.

NOW DO I WANT WEATHER HELM?

▲ Yes, now you want weather helm. Here are some adjustments to make:

With your sails:
Move the mainsail draft aft so that the curve is in the middle of the sail. As with any adjustment, always make small adjustments so you don't do too much. Tuning the boat is an art, not a science.

- Ease halyard, cunningham, outhaul.
- Increase vang and backstay.
- Pull traveler to windward (not above centerline) and trim the sheet.
- The telltales should be streaming straight back.

Move the jib draft aft
- Move jib lead aft.
- Ease the jib sheet.
- Tighten the halyard.
- The inside telltales should be lifting a bit and the outside telltales should be streaming straight back.

Looking at a
mainsail draft.

Stock Newport/Onne Van Der Wal

WEATHER HELM

With the crew
- Move the crew weight forward.

On the boat
- Move the mast base or position the mast with blocks forward, so that the mast rake is aft. Do not violate the rules of your class.
- Raise the centerboard.

If you take these steps in medium winds (5 to 10 knots), your weather helm should increase. Be sure to make any adjustment slowly, and never make more than one adjustment at a time. In technical terms, increasing your weather helm will move your CE aft and your CLR forward into alignment.

When the wind is under eight knots, moving the crew weight to leeward and keeping the traveler slightly to windward or above the center line helps keep the weather helm.

Notice what happens to the draft of the sails when you try some trim.

WOW, THIS IS HEAVY

▲ When the wind is over twelve knots, move the crew weight to windward and lower the traveler down to leeward. When the boat feels overpowered by the wind, another way to keep the boat balanced is to reduce the sail area.

With the sails:

Start with these steps. If they don't work, continue to <u>reverse</u> the steps that increase weather helm.

1. Move the mainsail draft forward.
   * Ease the sheet.
   * Ease the traveler to leeward.
   * Tighten the cunningham.
2. Move jib draft forward.
   * Trim the jib sheet.
   * Tighten the halyard.

With the crew:

   * Move the weight to windward and aft, hike out to reduce heel.

On the boat:

   * Lower the centerboard.
   * Increase the backstay.

Too much weather helm causes a dingy to capsize and a keel boat to round up into the wind. And too much lee helm is not safe either, since your boat could accidently gybe if you let go of the helm.

EVEN ON A KEELBOAT

▲ The bigger the boat you sail, the more controls there are to keep the mast upright. The babystay and running backstays are two such controls. The babystay is very useful in heavy air when sailing to windward and when sailing downwind with the spinnaker up. This is because the babystay prevents the mast from inverting.

Running backstays are also important since they control fore and aft bend of the mast. Increasing the tension of the running backstay on the windward side reduces mast bend and mast pumping (when the mast rocks back and forth — as when hitting a wave). Both the runner and backstay must be adjusted together so that the pulling forces do not compress the mast to the breaking point.

DEMASTED!

▲ Masts are not made to fall down. However, certain things can bring a mast down, usually at an inopportune moment.

Too much stress on the mast from the standing rigging tension, too many unsupported pieces, or the wrong pins holding the rigging to the boat — these are the main causes of demastings. Before you sail, make sure that all pins are the correct size and are not damaged or cracked. Also, be sure you are not over tensioning the rig with too much pressure on the stays.

5
TERMS
RACING RULES
IRPCAS

TERMS

ABANDONMENT

An abandoned race is one that is declared void at any time and that may be re-sailed.

BEARING AWAY

Altering course away from the wind until a yacht begins to gybe.

CLEAR ASTERN and CLEAR AHEAD; OVERLAP

A yacht is clear astern of another when her hull and equip ment in normal position are abaft an imaginary line projected abeam from the aftermost point of the other's hull and equipment in normal position. The other yacht is clear ahead.

The yachts overlap when neither is clear astern, or when, although one is clear astern, an intervening yacht overlaps both of them.

The terms clear astern, clear ahead, and overlap apply to yachts on opposite tacks only when they are subject to rule 42. For the purposes of rules 39.1, 39.2, and 40 only: an overlap does not exist unless the yachts are clearly within two overall lengths of the longer yacht, and an overlap that exists when the leeward yacht starts, or when one or both yachts completes a tack or a gybe, shall be regarded as beginning then.

CLOSE-HAULED

A yacht is close-hauled when sailing by the wind as close as she can lie with advantage in working to windward.

FINISHING

A yacht finishes when any part of her hull, or of her crew or equipment in normal position, crosses the finishing line in the direction of the course from the last mark, after fulfilling any penalty obligations under rule 52.2(b).

GYBING

A yacht begins to gybe at the moment when, with the wind aft, the foot of her mainsail crosses her center line, and completes the gybe when the mainsail has filled on the other tack.

INTERESTED PARTY

Anyone who stands to gain or lose as a result of a decision of a protest committee or who has a close personal interest in the result.

T E R M S

LEEWARD and WINDWARD

The leeward side of a yacht is that on which she is, or, when head to wind, was, carrying her mainsail. The opposite side is the windward side.

When neither of two yachts on the same tack is clear astern, the one on the leeward side of the other is the leeward yacht. The other is the windward yacht.

LUFFING

Altering course towards the wind.

MARK

A mark is any object specified in the sailing instructions that a yacht must round or pass on a required side. Ground tackle and any object accidentally or temporarily attached to the mark are not part of it.

MAST ABEAM

A windward yacht sailing no higher than a leeward yacht is mast abeam when her helmsman's line of sight abeam from his normal station is forward of the leeward yacht's mainmast.

A windward yacht sailing higher than a leeward yacht is mast abeam when her helmsman's line of sight abeam from his normal station would be, if she were sailing no higher, forward of the leeward yacht's mainmast.

OBSTRUCTION

An obstruction is any object, including a vessel under way, large enough to require a yacht, when more than one overall length away from it, to make a substantial alteration of course to pass on one side or the other, or any object that can be passed on one side only, including a buoy when the yacht in question cannot safely pass between it and the shoal or the object that it marks. The sailing instructions may prescribe that a specified area shall rank as an obstruction.

ON A TACK; STARBOARD TACK; PORT TACK

A yacht is on a tack except when she is tacking or gybing. A yacht is on the tack (starboard or port) corresponding to her windward side.

T E R M S

OVERLAP

See Clear Astern and Clear Ahead; Overlap.

PARTIES TO A PROTEST

(a) The protesting yacht, the protested yacht and any other yacht involved in the incident that might be penalized as a result of the protest;
(b) a yacht that has requested redress;
(c) the race committee when it is involved in a protest under rules 69(a) or 70; and
(d) a competitor who has been or is liable to be penalized.

POSTPONEMENT

A postponed race is one that is not started at its scheduled time and that can be sailed at any time the race committee may decide.

PROPER COURSE

A proper course is any course that a yacht might sail after the starting signal, in the absence of the other yachts affected, to finish as quickly as possible. There is no proper course before the starting signal.

PROTEST

An action taken by a yacht, race committee or protest committee to initiate a hearing on a possible infringement of a rule or a consideration of redress in accordance with rule 68, 69, or 70.

PROTEST COMMITTEE

The body appointed to hear and decide protests in accordance with rule 1.4.

RACING

A yacht is racing from her preparatory signal until she has either finished and cleared the finishing line and finishing marks or retired, or until the race has been postponed or abandoned, or a general recall has been signalled.

ROOM

Room is the space needed by a yacht to maneuver in a seamanlike manner in the prevailing conditions.

RULES

(a) These racing rules, including the definitions, preambles and the rules of an appendix when it applies;
(b) the prescriptions of the national authority concerned, when they apply;
(c) the sailing instructions;
(d) the class rules; and
(e) any other conditions governing the event.

SAILING

A yacht is sailing when using only the wind and water to increase, maintain or decrease her speed, with her crew adjusting the trim of sails and hull and performing other acts of seamanship.

STARTING

A yacht starts when, after fulfilling her penalty obligations, if any, under rule 51.1(c), and after her starting signal, any part of her hull, crew or equipment first crosses the starting line in the direction of the course to the first mark.

TACKING

A yacht is tacking from the moment she is beyond head to wind until she has borne away to a close-hauled course.

WINDWARD

See Leeward and Windward.

OTHER TERMS

We will be using terms that may be unfamiliar or new. Because these rules are in fact federal laws, exact definitions are important.

VESSEL

Every description of watercraft used or capable of being used as a means of transportation on the water.

MOTORBOAT

Any vessel propelled by machinery, including any sailing vessel under sail and power.

OTHER TERMS

SAILING VESSEL
Any vessel which is under sail alone, including any power vessel under sail alone.

UNDERWAY
Not at anchor, aground, or made fast to the shore.

DANGER ZONE
An arc of 112 degrees measured from dead ahead to off the starboard beam.

RIGHT-OF-WAY
The right and duty to maintain course and speed.

STAND-ON (PRIVILEGED) VESSEL
The vessel that has the right of-way.

GIVE-WAY (BURDENED) VESSEL
The vessel that must keep clear of the privileged vessel.

VISIBLE
Visible on a dark, clear night (when applied to lights).

SHORT BLAST (ON WHISTLE)
A blast of one to two seconds duration.

PROLONGED BLAST (ON WHISTLE)
A blast of four to six seconds duration.

UNDERSTANDING THE RULES OF THE ROAD

A word of encouragement: you will not be expected to quote all the rules of the road. However, no matter where you do your boating, others have the right to assume that you know what you are doing. Remember, when you take the wheel or tiller, there is a presumption of knowledge! If you fail to observe the rules, the fact that you did not know them will not be a valid defense. Navigation skills, like driving skills, are meaningless without a set of basic rules of the road. These rules are often common-sense guidelines. They supply uniform patterns for safe operating behavior; rules prevent accidents.

PLAYING BY THE RULES

▲ Since 1965, the International Yacht Racing Union has set rules that are adjusted by the United States Sailing Association or other national authorities. Local race committees can adjust the rules governing a particular race. The rules and any changes are usually referred to in sailing instructions. Before any competition, check all instruction and notices so that you play by the rules.

HOW YOU PLAY THE GAME

▲ The United States Sailing Association rule book completely details your responsibilities as a racing competitor. Competition is a fun and easy way to improve your sailing skills. It is extremely important that you have your own copy of the current racing rules and that you are familiar with any changes or prescriptions. Copies are free of charge when you join the United States Sailing Association and are updated or re-evaluated every four years. The following ideas are general explanations; to fully understand the rules, you need to go over your own copy of the rule book.

Play by the rules and avoid collisions.

Stock Newport/Skip Brown

PART I

FUNDAMENTAL RULES

A) RENDERING ASSISTANCE
Every yacht shall render all possible assistance to any vessel or person in peril, when in a position to do so.

B) COMPETITOR'S RESPONSIBILITIES
It shall be the sole responsibility of each yacht to decide whether or not to start or to continue to race. By participating in a race conducted under these rules, each competitor and yacht owner agrees: (i) to be governed by the rules; (ii) to accept the penalties imposed and other action taken in accordance with the rules, subject to the appeal and review procedures provided in them, as the final determination of any matter arising under the rules; and (iii) with respect to such a determination, not to resort to any court or tribunal not provided by the rules.

C) FAIR SAILING
A yacht, her owner and crew shall compete only by sailing, using their speed and skill, and, except in team racing, by individual effort, in compliance with the rules and in accordance with recognized principles of fair play and sportsmanship. A yacht may be penalized under this rule only in the case of a clear-cut violation of the above principles and only when no other rule applies, except rule 75.

D) ACCEPTING PENALTIES
A yacht that realizes she has infringed a rule while racing shall either retire promptly or accept an alternative penalty when so prescribed in the sailing instructions.

RACING RULES

Part II of the Racing rules deals with the organization and management for running a race, or regatta. This section details how the race should be governed, the sailing instructions, and generally what occurs before, during, and even after racing.

Part III covers the general requirements of the race. These requirements must be adhered to before the preparatory signal of the race as well as during the race.

Barbara Farquhar, US Sailing judge, at the Optimist Nationals.

Leeds Mitchell officiating a regatta.

Part IV is the most prominent section of the rules. This section applies when yachts intend to race. When any yacht is not racing, the International Regulations for Preventing Collisions at Sea governs the roadway for all power and sail boats.

THE RACING RULES

There are 17 rules in Part IV, divided into 3 sections. Obviously, for safety reasons, preventing collisions is truly important. But what if you, on port tack, had the room and opportunity to keep clear of a starboard tack boat?

RULE 36

▲ The first rule to consider in the below situation is rule 36. "A port tack yacht shall keep clear of a starboard tack yacht." Other rules that affect rule 36 are: rule 32, Serious Damage;

and rule 33, Contacts Between Yachts Racing. Unless otherwise stated in the sailing instructions, a starboard tack yacht must protest a port tack yacht for a collision if port tack did not exonerate herself, or take responsibility for hitting starboard tack. If port tack accepts a penalty, like sailing a 720° circle, then starboard tack can't protest port tack unless the damage to starboard tack is considered serious.

RULE 37

▲ Infringements of rule 37 refer to being clear ahead, clear astern, or overlapped. Keeping clear means not hitting another yacht. If you are overtaking a yacht to windward, you must allow the windward yacht room and opportunity to keep clear. Rules 35, 38, 39 and 40 can also effect rule 37.

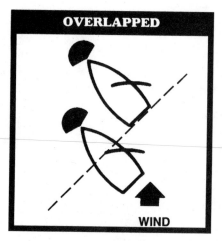

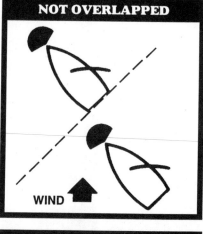

RULE 41

▲ Tacking or gybing too close to another yacht usually results in loud discussions between boats. The yacht doing the tacking or gybing has the onus in rule 41.3, or must prove to the protest committee that she completed the tack or gybe in accordance with rule 41.2. This means that the tacking or gybing yacht must give the sailing yacht ample room and opportunity to keep clear.

SECTION C

▲ Section C of Part IV are rules that apply at marks, obstacles, or other exceptions to the rules in Section B. Section C takes precedence over Section B, or overrides Section B's rules except for rule 35 Limitations on Altering Course.

RULE 42

▲ Some conditions apply to rule 42. When starting and clearing the starting area, the leeward yacht must not sail above the compass course to the mark or above close hauled. And when two yachts are beating on opposite tacks , one yacht must tack to round the mark or avoid the obstruction.

RULE 43

▲ Hailing and Responding are a part of rule 43. It is wise to hail a yacht that may need the room and opportunity to keep clear of your yacht. This not only prevents a collision, but it also serves as a common courtesy. You never know when the situation may be reversed.

RACING RULES

RULE 52

▲ Although only a few racing rules are covered here, there are a lot more rules to consider and understand before you race so that you play the game safely and fairly. Rule 52, Part V, has been recently changed. This rule addresses touching a mark. To exonerate yourself, the rule change states that as soon as possible, sailing well clear, you must immediately make one complete 360 degree turn including one tack and one gybe.

Section VI handles protests, penalties and appeals. According to rule 68.1, any yacht has the right to protest another yacht, except that if a yacht is involved in a violation of a rule in Park IV, only the yachts involved or a witnessing yacht can protest. There are rules that specify the who, what, where, when, why and how of protests. If the outcome of the protest is still disputed, the protest can be appealed to the National Authority for a final decision.

PART II

▲ While the racing rules are important to understand for a safe and fair competition, the International Regulations for Preventing Collisions at Sea govern all vessels on the water.

FOLLOW THE RULES

▲ There are simple rules to follow when boating. Most federal, state and local waterways have specific rules to follow; contact the Coast Guard or local boating authorities.

IRPCAS

In general, speeding in crowded areas, operating any vessel while under the influence of drugs or alcohol, driving through or near hazardous areas, and deliberately cutting through regattas or parades are not permitted, since they endanger people and boats. Most states are adopting these rules as laws and violations punishable by fines or even jail. Other rules include not mooring to navigational aids and not polluting or littering any beach, waterway, or marshland.

THE RIGHT-OF-WAY

▲ While boating, one vessel has the right-of-way while the other vessel must give way. Below are certain situations showing the **privileged vessel** and the **burdened vessel**. Common sense is truly important in avoiding a collision. By signalling the other boat, you can make your intentions known. The best advice is to simply stay out of the way of bigger vessels, always be visible and/or heard, constantly watch for other vessels, and use the appropriate night lights when boating from sunset to sunrise.

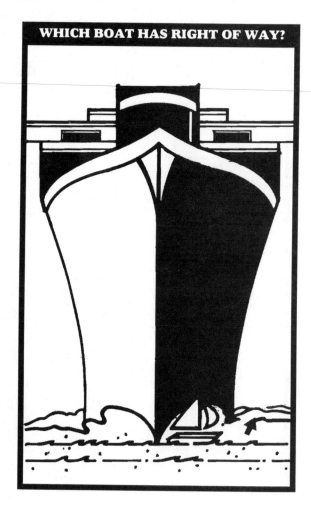

WHICH BOAT HAS RIGHT OF WAY?

IRPCAS

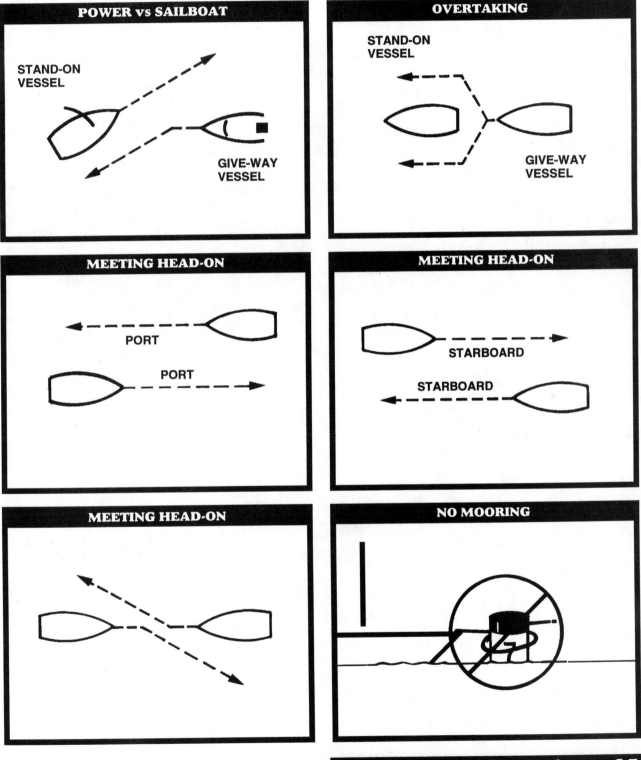

POWER vs SAILBOAT

STAND-ON VESSEL

GIVE-WAY VESSEL

OVERTAKING

STAND-ON VESSEL

GIVE-WAY VESSEL

MEETING HEAD-ON

PORT

PORT

MEETING HEAD-ON

STARBOARD

STARBOARD

MEETING HEAD-ON

NO MOORING

 **SKIPPERING
DUTIES
DIALOGUE
WINDWARD MARK
REACHING
GYBE MARK
LEEWARD MARK
WORKING TOGETHER**

ART IN A CRAFT

▲ The art of skippering and crewing is more complex than just driving the boat. If you are sailing with an inexperienced crew, make sure they understand any maneuver before it is made and that all activities are well coordinated. Tell the crew what will happen and how it will happen.

Even if the situation does not go according to plan, never get mad. Yelling, pouting or insulting remarks won't get the job done. Remember that the skipper makes the decisions and

A skipper and crew must work together to make the boat sail well.

always needs to update the crew on any changes. The skipper also has to take all safety precautions and make sure that everyone on board knows what to do in an emergency.

Skippers and crew must communicate and practice situations continuously. If you've heard the saying "he who makes the

DUTIES

fewest mistakes wins," you know that no matter how fast the boat sails, you cannot win a race or arrive at a destination safely with poor helming or crewing. Look at the lists of skipper and crew duties, discuss each point with your partners and use practice sessions to perfect your skills.

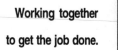

Working together

to get the job done.

GENERAL DUTIES OF THE SKIPPER

- Be responsible for the boat's condition.
- Choose a capable crew.
- Be organized before, during, and after an event.
- Be a team leader and player.
- Set confident goals and never expect more than the crew can handle. Always have a positive attitude.
- Be alert to changes in wind, performance, etc.
- Make sure the crew understands the maneuvers.

GENERAL DUTIES OF THE CREW

- Handle the sails and their controls.
- Set priorities of jobs to be done.
- Be enthusiastic under pressure.
- Contribute during a crisis.

Good communication is essential to getting the job done.

- Respond to the skipper's decisions.
- Be alert to changes in wind, performance, weather and other boats.
- Determine tactical information and discuss your ideas with the skipper.

6

AND THE SKIPPER SAYS...

▲ Clear commands keep communication quick and easy.

- "Ready to Tack," "Ready to Gybe" or "Ready About"
- "Tacking" or "Gybing" or "Hard a Lee"
- "Trim Jib" or "Ease Sheets"
- "Head Up" or "Head Down"
- "Don't Pinch" or "Footing"
- "Hoist the _____ Sail" or "Drop the _____ Sail"
- "Let Go" or "Fend Off"

On the first beat.

The crew should acknowledge the commands either by repeating the command or simply saying "Ready to _____."
Remember that a successful team effort is a combination of skipper and crew input.

DUTIES

WHO DOES WHAT WHEN...

SKIPPER AND CREW

Before the race:

Check the boat, making sure that everything is set properly and fittings are adjusted. Check all gear. Attend the skipper's meeting together; be sure you understand your sailing instructions and obligations. Don't forget to check the equipment list in the "GO" section, or make your own list. Your preparations could make the difference between winning and losing a race.

Before the start:

SKIPPER

- Know the race course and understand what might happen if the wind changes directions. Know which mark you will need to head toward.
- Know the wind and weather conditions. Check the tides and determine how the tides may help or hinder you.

CREW

- Check the wind direction more than once. Write down starboard and port lifts, knocks, and standard headings. These will help the skipper determine when to tack or gybe.
- Discuss your desired position at the start of the race and where you want to be on the start line.

TECHNICAL CONSIDERATIONS

- Make sure the rig is tuned.
- Make sure the boat doesn't heel too much; this could mean there is too much weather helm. If the skipper turns the rudder too often, this will actually cause the boat to brake.
- Check sail controls (vang, cunningham, traveller, etc.) to keep the sails flat or full depending upon the conditions.
- Address wind puffs or lulls by hiking out or in; handle a long puff or lull with mainsheet and jib sheet adjustments.

The first beat:

SKIPPER
- Get clear air after the start on the favored side of the course.
- Tack the boat smoothly.
- Achieve maximum speed while pointing.

CREW
- Check that sails are trimmed properly at all times.
- Don't take too long to trim in the sails after tacking.
- Make sure that crew weight is properly distributed.

Common mistakes made by the skipper or crew:

- Over-sheeting the sails.
- The crew blocking the skipper's vision.
- Having no communication.
- Having sails too full and not trimming them according to the telltales.
- Not knowing when to add or ease the controls such as the cunningham, vang, etc.

ROUNDING THE MARK

▲ Communication is the key to smooth mark roundings. Approaching the windward mark on starboard allows maximum time for the crew to prepare the pole and raise the chute. A port-tack approach works when you won't infringe on the rules and when you have the space you need to tack, prepare the pole, ready the spinnaker and set the sail.

Rounding the windward mark.

SKIPPER
- Ease controls such as the cunningham, outhaul, etc.
- Decide when to take down the spinnaker, especially if conditions are not appropriate.
- Raise the centerboard to reach position.

CREW
- Set the pole.
- Ready and raise the spinnaker, lower the jib.
- Take the sheet and guy.

REACHING

6

REACHING

SKIPPER
- Check the trim and draft of the main.
- Decide on your proper heel.

CREW
- Never cleat the spinnaker sheet; constantly adjust it.
- Cleat the guy and check its position regularly.
- As the wind builds, adjust the controls.
- Call wind gusts or waves for planing or surfing.

Sailing fast on a

reach.

GYBE MARK

THE GYBE MARK

Usually you will need to gybe. Communication is essential for a smooth rounding.

SKIPPER
- Prepare early, adjust the controls and steer a course that will turn the boat inside the sail.
- Don't gybe while surfing or when the crew is not ready.

CREW
- Do your job smoothly.
- Be careful not to collapse the spinnaker.
- Go to your new position quickly and settle the boat.

Getting ready to gybe.

LEEWARD MARK

THE LEEWARD MARK

SKIPPER
- About 5 to 10 boat lengths before rounding the leeward mark, note any wind shifts, weather and/or mark changes.
- Put controls back on.
- Ease centerboard down.

CREW
- Give the sheet and guy to the skipper, raise the jib, take down the pole and, finally, the spinnaker.
- Trim the sails and make adjustments.

Oops!

UNITED WE STAND, DIVIDED WE FALL

▲ Once more, the keys to successful sailing and racing are communication and practice. Know your jobs and try different positions occasionally. In order to win, you must be prepared mentally and physically to avoid breakdowns. Also, don't forget to have fun!

 **TERMS**
SAILS
TELL TALES
SURFING
GYBING

T E R M S

BARBERHAUL
A line attached to the jib; it moves the jib lead inboard or outboard.

BATTEN
A flat stick that supports the leech of a sail.

BROACH
What happens when the boat rounds up toward the wind.

CAMBER
A curved shape that shows the fullness of a sail.

CHORD
An imaginary line connecting the entry and exit areas of a sail; it shows the amount of fullness.

DOWNHAUL
A line attached to the spinnaker pole; it keeps the pole stable and prevents it from angling up.

DRAFT
The convex area of a sail, usually referred to as camber.

ENTRY
The curve of the leading edge of a sail. (The leading edge is the part that the wind hits first.)

EXIT
The leech area, where the airflow leaves the sail.

FULLNESS
The depth, belly or sag of a sail.

GUY
A line attached to the spinnaker pole; it controls the fore and aft position of the spinnaker pole.

KNOCK
Heading away from the wind.

LIFT
Heading up into the wind.

T E R M S

7

PLANE

When the lifting force of the boat, usually when on a reach, supports the boat so that the boat sails on top of the water, not through the water.

POINT

The ability to get closer to the wind.

SLOT

The vertical area between the main and the jib.

SPINNAKER SHEET

A line attached to the spinnaker; it controls the trim.

STALL

When an increase in drag and a decrease in lift stops the smooth flow of air around a foil or sail.

SURFING

Like planing except that the boat is moving down a wave.

TELLTALES

Yarn or strings attached to the sail; they show the direction of the airflow.

TOPPING LIFT

A line on the spinnaker pole that raises and lowers it.

TWIST

When the upper and lower portions of the sails are trimmed at different angles to each other. You can see this when you look from the bottom to the top of the sail.

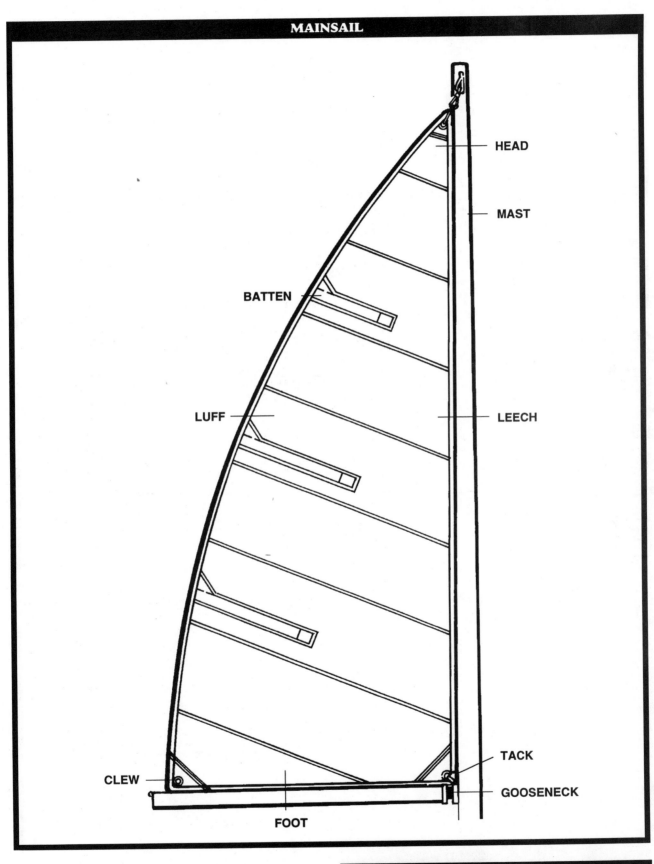

HEAD

MAST

BATTEN

LUFF

LEECH

TACK

CLEW

GOOSENECK

FOOT

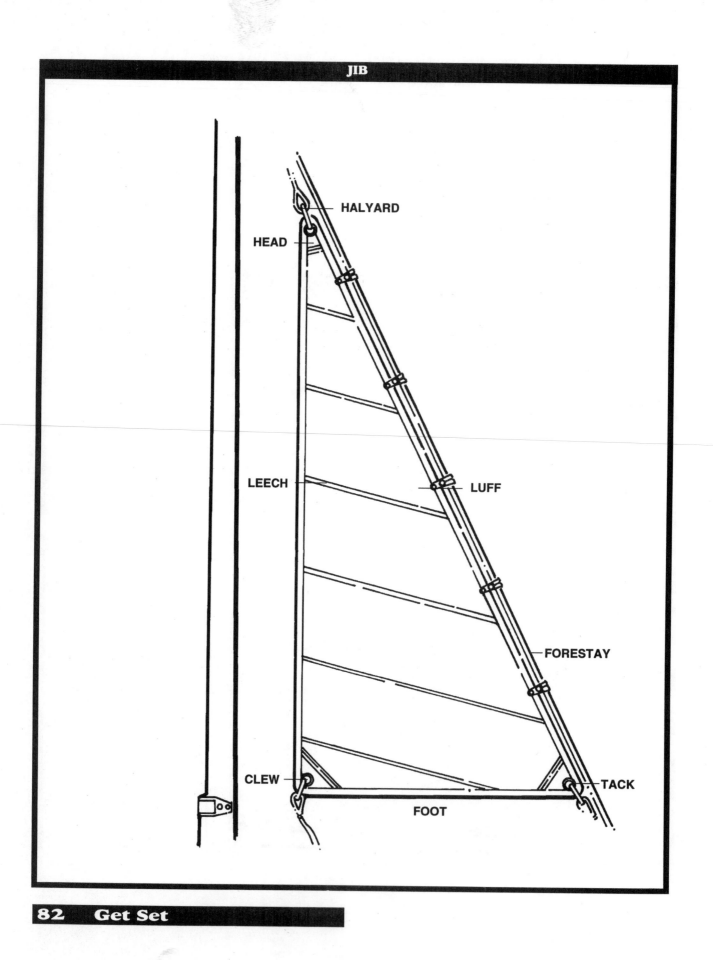

HALYARD

HEAD

LEECH

LUFF

FORESTAY

CLEW

TACK

FOOT

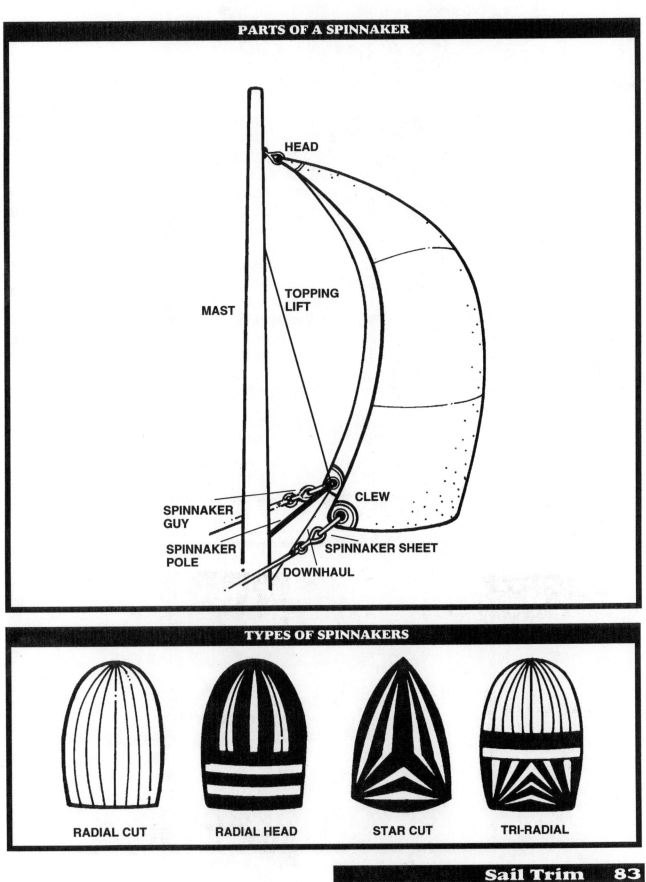

HEAD

MAST

TOPPING
LIFT

SPINNAKER
GUY

SPINNAKER
POLE

CLEW

DOWNHAUL

SPINNAKER SHEET

TYPES OF SPINNAKERS

RADIAL CUT

RADIAL HEAD

STAR CUT

TRI-RADIAL

SAILS

7

▲ Technically, the development of sails, sail material, and design continue to revolutionize our sport. Sailmakers have learned how to build certain shapes into a sail, making it perform better and last longer. When sailing, you need to be able to change the shape of the sails in relation to the direction of the wind. We all know how slow a main trimmed for an upwind course can be on a downwind leg.

With computers, designers can now show how a sail shape will perform at any point of sail before it is even made. Because there is a high monetary price to pay for technology, some class organizations limit the number of sails and the type of sail material used. This keeps the class updated on advances, but still affordable and enjoyable.

THE "MAIN" IDEA

▲ Depending on the sophistication of a boat, there can be as many as 10 separate controls for the mainsail! Each has a specific function. The easiest way to tell if the main is properly trimmed is to make sure that the **draft** is centered and the **telltales** are flying back. Here are some mainsail controls and reasons for using them.

S A I L S

VANG

The boom vang keeps the boom from rising and tensions the mainsail leech, especially when sailing a downwind course.

VANG SHEETING

Tensioning the vang when sailing upwind helps to control the mainsheet during medium to heavy air. This keeps the mainsail from having too much **twist**. Also, if the main is all the way to leeward on the traveller, vang sheeting aids trim.

OUTHAUL

The outhaul controls the amount of tension on the foot of the sail. In heavier air, a flat sail is preferred to one with too much **camber**. The reverse is true in lighter winds.

CUNNINGHAM

This control flattens the luff of the sail, reduces the camber, and moves the draft forward. Too much cunningham twists the top part of the sail. Tighten the cunningham just enough so that luff wrinkles are removed.

HALYARD

Obviously, the halyard raises and lowers the sail, but it also controls the amount of fullness. The more tension, the less full the sail becomes.

TRAVELLER

The traveller controls the boom and the twist of the mainsail. Moving the boom along the traveller has almost the same effect as trimming or easing the mainsheet. Once the main is completely trimmed, it's preferable to adjust the traveller since it prevents the boom from moving vertically.

BACKSTAY

Tensioning the backstay does two jobs. It flattens the mainsail and the jib.

LEECH CORD

This control keeps the leech from fluttering. Too much leech-cord tension cups the sail and makes the **exit area** inefficient.

S A I L S

7

▲ When sailing to windward, you don't want to be overpowered — and certainly not capsized. In flat water, you might want to point a little higher into the wind. When the conditions are wavy, you might want to power through the waves by easing the main down on the traveller. Sail twist allows wind to behave the same from the top of the sail to the bottom. In heavy air, having twist lets the leech fall off, reducing the boat's heel. The camber, or draft, of the sail should be centered. A recent trend in sailing is to use a full-battened main to keep a continuous shape and prevent wear and tear when the main is luffed.

SAIL SHAPE (MAIN)

▲ When you're going upwind, use the following guide. When sailing downwind during medium or heavy air, ease the sail controls to keep the mainsail full.

Light Air
(0-3 knots)

- Use the controls lightly if at all.
- Keep the draft in the middle of the sail.
- Center the traveller — even a bit to windward to add pointing ability.

Medium Air
(8-15 knots)

- As the wind builds, use more controls. Increase outhaul, increase halyard tension, increase vang and increase cunningham.
- Ease the traveller down to depower during puffs and bring it up in the lulls.
- Put on the backstay.
- Keep the draft in the middle of the sail.

Heavy Air
(over 15 knots)

- Completely tension the outhaul, cunningham, vang, backstay and halyard.
- Ease the traveller to leeward to depower the boat. After easing the traveller completely, ease the sheet to keep the boat from heeling too much.
- Remember that in heavy air, a flat sail is a fast sail. A flat sail holds less wind and keeps the boat from heeling too much, reducing the amount of drag.

THE JIB

▲ The jib also has many controls to keep you sailing fast. Controls such as the halyard, sail cloth, jib lead and actual trim all determine the draft or fullness of the sail. The jib and main must work together to prevent air brakes. An air brake occurs when the **slot** lacks a consistent shape.

The best way to determine if the sail is trimmed correctly is to look at the telltales. If the telltales are moving at the same time, or "breaking evenly," the jib is trimmed properly. If the bottom telltale breaks first, try moving the jib lead aft. If the top telltale breaks first, move the jib lead forward.

S A I L S

7

Light Air
(0-8 knots)

- Keep very small wrinkles along the luff.
- Keep the jib lead forward of the neutral position. The telltales should be breaking evenly.
- Remember that in light air the fastest sail is a fuller sail, with the boat not pointing too high (known as pinching).

Medium to
Heavy Air

(9-25+ knots)

- Keep the halyard tensioned.
- Make sure other controls are on.
- Move the lead aft so that the draft remains centered.
- Use the telltales as a guide.

If you are sailing a fetch or are in between close-hauled and a reach, you may want to barberhaul the jib to move the sail outboard. This adds fullness to the sail.

LOOK, LISTEN, AND FEEL

▲ Both the jib and the main have entry and exit areas. The best way to maximize the shapes of both sails is to simply not stall. **Stalling** occurs when the sails are trimmed too tight, when the boat is pointed too high during a **lift** or when the boat is sailed too low on a **knock**. Once again, the key is to look at the telltales, listen for luffing and get a feel for the boat when it heels too much.

Jib telltales show you if the draft is in the right place, if the sail is trimmed properly, if you are lifted or if you are knocked.

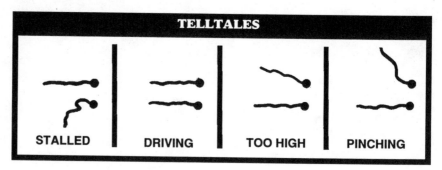

TELLTALES

STALLED   DRIVING   TOO HIGH   PINCHING

Stock Newport/Onne Van Der Wal

CHUTE, YES!

▲ Spinnakers are not as complicated to use as you might think. There are a few general principles to remember. Once you have the spinnaker up, flying it is easy.

7

First
Always set the pole on the windward side of the boat. Sometimes you might have to gybe first, then set the pole on the new windward side of the boat.

Second
The pole height, set with the **topping lift**, includes both the inboard (on the mast) and the outboard (where the **guy** is attached) ends. Make both spinnaker clews even horizontally. Also, you want the spinnaker curls along the luff to be breaking near the top of the sail. Raising or lowering the pole determines where the curl will occur.

Third
The pole position is usually at a 90-degree angle to the wind. Also keep the **downhaul** tensioned, which prevents the spinnaker from bouncing around.

Fourth
Trim or ease the spinnaker sheet according to the luff. Expect a fold or curl of one to three panels of the sail, depending on the size of the boat and the amount of wind. Constantly trim the spinnaker according to wind shifts or oscillations. Again, keep the draft of the spinnaker in the center.

Fifth
If the winds are heavy or the boat feels like it will **broach**, "choke" the spinnaker by moving the leads to the middle of the boat. Another way to control the spinnaker is to over-square the pole by trimming it more than 90 degrees to the wind. This flattens the lower part of the spinnaker.

Sixth
Never sail dead downwind since the boat will want to gybe.

▲ Using the spinnaker in heavy weather while running downwind means trying to keep the boat as upright as possible and ready to **plane**. The helmsperson needs to be balanced properly to anticipate the waves and wind gusts. Make sure that the main is eased enough. If the boat begins to broach, ease the spinnaker sheet, ease the main, control the heel and head down; being careful not to roll to leeward too much. Planing increases the boat's normal speed. Once the wind lifts the bow over the wave, the boat will stay on top of the water. If the wind is strong enough, a boat can plane upwind or downwind, although planing usually occurs on a reach when the wind gusts.

PLANING AND SURFING

SURFING

PLANING

SURF 'ER DUDE

▲ In order to **surf**, or stay on the front of a wave to gain maximum speed, both the skipper and the crew trim their sails slightly and ease out as the wave hits the stern of the boat. Crew weight should be aft, allowing the bow to rise.

7

CAN'T FILL

If your spinnaker can't fill, try heading up to a reach.

TWISTED

The spinnaker was twisted during packing. Try lowering the halyard a few inches or gently tug on leech or lower the spinnaker and untwist.

GYBE HO!

▲ Gybing is a simple procedure, no matter the wind's strength. Practice makes perfect, and following these steps will ensure a smooth, controlled gybe.

- Helmsperson and crew move to the center of the boat.

- Helmsperson keeps the main directly at the center of the boat, with virtually no wind hitting the mainsail.

- Crew removes the pole as the boat is headed dead downwind.

- The boat turns slowly inside of the spinnaker with the spinnaker remaining full during the entire gybe.

- The pole is then attached to the new side.

- The mainsail is released to the new side with the crew balancing the boat.

8

TERMS
TACTICS
VMG
STARTING

FIRST BEAT
REACHING
RUNNING
MISTAKES

T E R M S

BARGING   When starting, a boat approaches the windward starting area from a windward position outside the starting area.

BLANKET or BAD AIR   Disturbed airflow caused by a wind shadow either from other boats, an island or an obstruction.

CLEAR AIR   Undisturbed airflow.

COVER   Watching the competition while trying to keep your boat between the mark and your competition.

FAVORED   The end of the starting or finish line that is the closest to your boat.

KNOCKED   As the wind shifts or oscillates, the boat sails away from the previous course.

LAYLINE   An imaginary line showing the port and starboard course boundaries.

LEE BOW   A wind shadow that occurs when a leeward boat disturbs the airflow of a windward boat.

OSCILLATION   A temporary change in the wind direction.

OVERSTOOD   Sailing beyond the layline.

T E R M S

8

POLAR DIAGRAM	A series of calculations that determine target speeds for various wind speeds.
RHUMBLINE	An imaginary line showing the direct course to the mark.
SQUARE	A term referring to a starting line or finish line that does not have a favored end.
TARGET SPEED	The maximum boat speed.
VELOCITY MADE GOOD (VMG)	A calculation showing the angular relationship between the boat, the true wind and the apparent sailing direction.
WIND SHIFT	A steady change in wind direction.

Whether you are only going out for a short cruise around the harbor or you are going to spend the day racing, you need a tactical plan. Tactics for a simple cruise are not so demanding as racing tactics.

WHAT'S THE GAME PLAN?

▲ **Tactics** are the ideas behind a game plan, helping you to formulate a strategy. Knowing different sailing tactics is just one way to be a successful racer. Even if your boat is fast and your crew efficient, going to the wrong side of the race course could put you dead last. So have a game plan and use it — you will be guaranteed success!

A polar diagram shows the boat's speed relative to the wind speed. The point where the boat hits the black line marks the boat's top speed. Notice that there is no black line at the top of the polar diagram. That's because you can't sail directly into the wind.

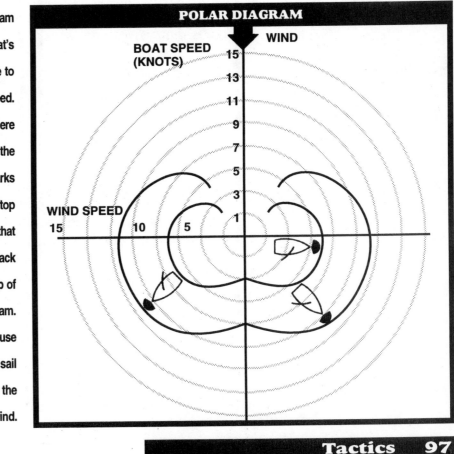

POLAR DIAGRAM

BOAT SPEED (KNOTS)

WIND

15
13
11
9
7
5
3
1

WIND SPEED

15   10   5

BIG VERSUS LITTLE

▲ "Big" boat tactics are similar to "little" boat tactics. The difference is the use of technology and computers. For many years, big boats have used electronic equipment — especially knot meters and wind indicators — to help determine their racing tactics.

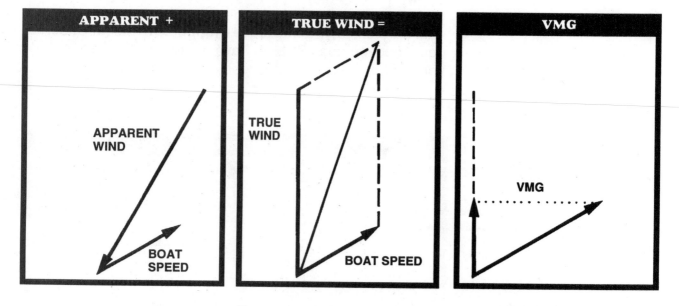

Boat speed, the true and apparent wind speed and direction can be programmed into a computer to determine functions such as **velocity made good (VMG)**, **target speed**, current position, or your **course over the ground**.

Velocity made good, your course over ground, and target speed are three functions that can be calculated for the upwind and downwind legs of the course. Essentially, VMG

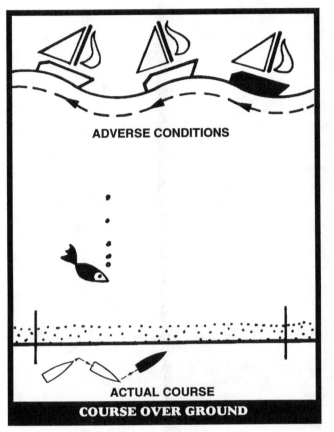

ADVERSE CONDITIONS

ACTUAL COURSE

COURSE OVER GROUND

finds the boat's speed according to the true wind and the boat's apparent sailing direction angles. Then the computer tells if the boat is sailing at the optimum angle and if the boat should be headed up or down.

The boat's target speed can tell the helmsperson or crew whether the boat is sailing as fast as possible. Usually, the target speed is a result of a polar coordinate on a polar diagram, computed for a particular wind speed.

The course over the ground is an actual account of how the boat is moving against a current or waves. For example, if a boat is traveling five knots an hour and has an adverse current pushing the boat backwards at two knots per hour, the actual course over the ground for the hour would be three nautical miles. Think about the opposite situation: a boat sailing with a two-knot current traveling in the same direction as the boat. The course over ground would be quite significant.

BE PREPARED

▲ Setting up a strategy means more than just deciding to race. It means making sure you have a crew, that your boat is ready to race and that everything works on your boat. Remember that little clevis pin that holds up the mast? The race course is not the place to find out that this little pin snaps under pressure.

Other preparations include knowing where to stay at away regattas; how the boat will get to the regatta; and what the crew will eat. A hungry or thirsty crew can cause a mutiny!

Most big boats use compasses, Loran, wind indicators or computers to determine their initial on-the-water tactics. Just because you don't have a computer (let alone a compass) you can still form a race strategy.

Before the start, take time to:

- Put the boat head-to-wind and luff the sails. The direction the bow takes is the side of the course that is currently favored. This can be difficult to do in heavy air and big waves.
- Check the starting line to find out how the race committee set the starting line in relation to the windward mark. Is one end favored or closer ?
- Check again a few minutes before the start.
- Check the current at the start line. Will it push you over the line?
- Another way to determine the favored end of the starting line is to: Sail directly down the starting line from the committee boat to the starting pin. Take a compass bearing, then write it and the reciprocal down. Take a true

reading. Subtract 90 degrees from the true wind. If the numbers are equal, the line is square. If the compass number is larger, the starboard end is favored. If the compass number is smaller, the port end is favored.

- Go upwind, look around. Are other boats sailing well in relation to you?
- Check the wind for shifts or oscillations. Does one area of the race course have more wind than another?
- Know the water. Where is the favorable current going? Will large waves help you or hurt you? Is the sea breeze going to come up from one particular direction?
- Fifteen to 30 seconds before the start, get into position to get clear air. It is almost more important to have clear air than the best start.
- Tell your crew the strategy. For example, say, "We are going to start on the starboard end of line. Our first tack will be when the wind knocks us 10 degrees from our average course."

At the start, be sure you are at full speed and that you are not leebowed. Also make sure that a boat to windward will not steamroll over you or force you over the starting line early.

FIRST BEAT

RECOVERING FROM A BAD START

▲ You were over early; you were **barging;** or you arrived at the start late. It's OK! The key is to recover, not let this ruin the day and sail on according to your game plan.

THE FIRST BEAT

▲ **Wind shifts**, **oscillations** and encounters with other boats determine when and if you should tack. Sometimes a wind shift lasts only a few seconds, and if you tack too soon into the shift, you could lose boat lengths. If you don't have a compass, use objects on the shore to see whether you have been lifted or knocked. If another boat is on the same tack and you

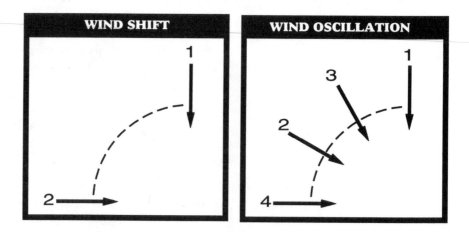

are lifted, the inside boat has the advantage. If you are sailing on a knocked course, the outside boat gains the advantage.

An oscillation is a shift that goes from, say, 100 degrees to 120 degrees, back to 100 degrees, then to 80 degrees. You can gain boat lengths by knowing how an oscillation could help you — such as giving you an opportunity to tack on the knock position of the oscillation. If the wind is gusting, don't tack once you sail into the gust. Since the apparent wind speed increases in a gust, this appears as a lift. The reverse is also true: sail into a lull, and the apparent wind speed drops, showing a knock. This event is called a velocity lift or a velocity knock.

FIRST BEAT

Be sure you sail in clear air. Sailing in disturbed air, or bad air, is slow since you are in the wind shadow of another boat or object. If you cannot tack to clear your air, foot the boat by sailing a course just a bit away from the boat or object that's giving you bad air until your air becomes clear.

How do you ensure a good first beat? Sail as fast as possible to the first mark, play the favorable wind shifts or oscillations, avoid collisions and the mark laylines.

Do you cross or duck? If you are on port and:

- are equal in speed and distance, obey the rules. Tack if you are on the unfavored tack, duck the starboard boat if you are on the favored tack.
- are a bit faster, tack to leebow if room and opportunity to cross are not available.

This is a tricky situtation because one boat is running and one is beating. What would you do in this situation? Check the rules to find out.

Things to remember as you approach a mark:
- Never go to a layline unless there are no wind shifts or currents. Also be sure you have not overstood the mark.
- If you are bunched up at the mark, know your rights and be in a position to get clear air.

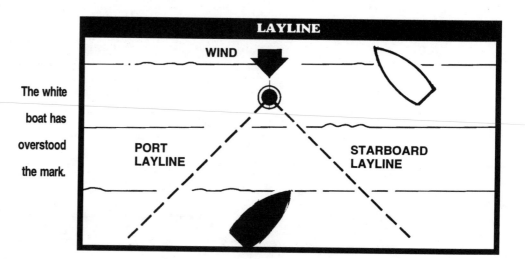

The white boat has overstood the mark.

THE REACH

▲The reach is usually a straight line to the next mark. Factors like tides and currents need to be considered, but, again, getting clear air is essential.

One tactical rule to remember is head up in lulls, head down in the puffs for maximum speed. Sometimes, you may get challenged or will challenge a competitor by luffing.

THE GYBE MARK

▲ Position the boat so that you have the inside spot at the gybe mark.

• Know the overlap rules, especially Rule 42, which tells you what to do two-boat lengths from the mark.

• Keep the spinnaker full while rounding the mark smoothly.

Gybing can be a tricky experience. As part of your pre-race strategy, practice gybing. Make absolutely sure that each crew member knows his or her job and knows how to complete the job under stressful conditions.

GYBING

RUNNING

THE RUN

▲ If your courseon the run is dead down, use a strategy of downwind tacking (really gybing) on shifts. The tactical rule is opposite of the upwind tactical rule: when a persistent shift occurs, gybe away from the shift. Again, use the waves and current to your favor. If you are taking down the spinnaker, have the job completed before rounding the mark so the rounding to windward is as smooth and error-free as possible.

GOING UP AGAIN

▲ Before going back up to windward, did you do something that worked well during the last beat? Or should you change the game plan? Has there been any shift in the current or wind? Do you need to cover your competition more effectively?

FINALLY FINISHING

You are neck and neck with another boat. What do you do?

* Find the shortest distance to mark.
* Cover or block your opponent.

RACING IN A SERIES

▲ Racing in a series of regattas is exhilarating. The series could be once a week for the entire summer or a weekend event that determines a national championship. Having a series strategy keeps the regatta fun and well organized. And just because you finished poorly in one race does not mean that you can't recover and win the series. Rest assured, everyone has had at least one horrible, not-worth-mentioning race.

Oops!

COMMON TACTICAL MISTAKES

- Tacking too much
- Not sailing the shortest distance between two points
- Not covering the competition
- Not going as fast as possible
- Taking too many risks
- Not sailing conservatively
- Having a poor attitude
- Making too many crewing errors
- Turning too fast or too tight at marks
- Losing sight of the competition
- Failing to consolidate tacks (usually the result of sailing to one layline)

9

PRACTICE

IT'S PRACTICAL

▲ Practice lets you make a habit out of a skill. Sailing practice means having a fun and enjoyable time while keeping your skills up to date. A sailor going out for a pleasure cruise needs to be just as prepared as the racing sailor. Knowing exactly what to do can make any emergency situation calmer, safer and easier to control.

Practice makes
perfect!

Stock Newport/Onne Van Der Wal

BOAT HANDLING

▲ Practice the following skills on a continual basis. In time they will become second nature.

Tacking

Although you might be familiar with sailing a figure eight, a triangle or sailing in a circle, try a slalom course. Use at least five marks set to windward. Practice tacking upwind and gybing downwind.

Roll Tacking

Once you are comfortable with tacking, try roll tacking. This is the most efficient way to tack a whether big or small boat in light to medium air.

These sailors are simply practicing rolling.

PRACTICE

Roll Gybing Same as roll tacking but for downwind. Make sure both roll tacking and roll gybing are done smoothly.

Man Overboard Use an old life jacket, a float or a buoy to practice man-overboard drills. Practice situations where the skipper or crew fall overboard.

Capsizing Never practice this alone. Try this skill with the boat tethered to an anchor. Turtling the boat might damage the mast so use a life jacket tied to the top. Then discuss the procedures for righting a turtled boat.

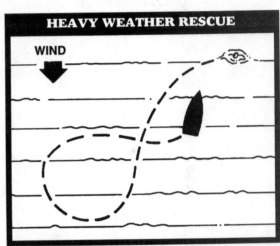

HEAVY WEATHER RESCUE

WIND

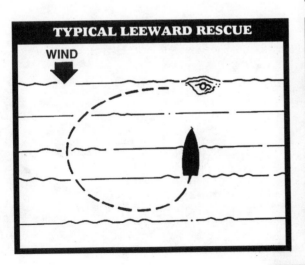

TYPICAL LEEWARD RESCUE

WIND

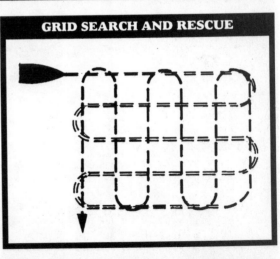

GRID SEARCH AND RESCUE

PRACTICE

9

Timing Time yourself doing any of the previous drills. Time yourself going between two marks. Can you go faster?

Change If you usually crew on the boat, try skippering. You should know how to perform every function on the boat.

Seamanship This includes docking, anchoring, sailing without a rudder, and towing the boat.

Practice any skills that are new to you. A sailing practice is meant to improve your basic skills. This is extremely important, since practice really does make perfect.

PRACTICE

10

TERMS
SEAMANSHIP
KNOTS
HARDWARE
DOCK
ANCHORING

STORMY SEAS
NAVIGATION
EMERGENCIES
PFD
SAFETY

T E R M S

ANCHOR	Anything that secures a boat to the bottom.
ANCHORAGE	A specific place good for anchoring. Anchorages are usually noted on nautical charts.
BEARING	The compass course of an object, from the boat or buoy.
BUOY	A floating mark to indicate a waterway entrance, a shoal or other aid to navigation.
CHART	A map of a body of water.
DRAG	Drag happens after anchoring, when the anchor does not sufficiently hold, causing the boat to drift.
HARBOR of REFUGE	A harbor or port that is the safest place to anchor your boat during a storm.
HEADING	The direction in which the boat is going, according to the compass course.
LYING at ANCHOR	When the anchor holds.

T E R M S

10

MAGNETIC DEVIATION

The compass difference between the boat's magnetic field and the Earth's magnetic field. A boat's compass can be "swung" to eliminate this deviation.

MAGNETIC VARIATION

The difference between the true north pole or south pole and the magnetic north pole or south pole.

POSITION

A latitude parallel and a longitude meridian pinpointing a specific location. Both latitudes and longitude are measured in degrees (°), minutes ('), and seconds or tenths of minutes.

RANGE

A fixed landmark used for exact steering.

RODE

The total amount of anchor line used.

SCOPE

The ratio of anchor line you use to the depth of the water. The ratio is usually seven feet of anchor line to each foot of water depth, but can change to three-to-one or even ten-to-one depending upon conditions.

SWING

When a boat pivots around the anchor as it lies at anchor.

WEIGHING ANCHOR

Leaving the anchorage.

SEAMANSHIP

WHAT IS SEAMANSHIP?

▲ There are many tasks involved in seamanship:

- Tying knots
- Whipping & splicing lines
- Using the deck hardware
- Docking the boat
- Anchoring
- Being prepared for storms
- Knowing what to do in emergencies
- Navigational techniques

Most seamanship tasks are things you learn when you first begin to sail. More advanced sailors continuously learn about being prepared — and that's precisely what this chapter is about. Have you practiced emergency procedures? Are you sure you can tie a bowline?

KNUTS ABOUT KNOTS

▲ Knot tying was a part of seamanship from the day the first sailor took to the water. The first ropes were made of vines or animal hides. Gradually, the ropes were twisted or braided to strengthen their fibers, and ropes became a useful part of everyday living. Today, ropes or lines are made of many types of materials — cotton, nylon, Kevlar or Dacron.

There are literally thousands of ways to tie a knot. The following, are the most common knots used in sailing. Each has its own purpose and holding power.

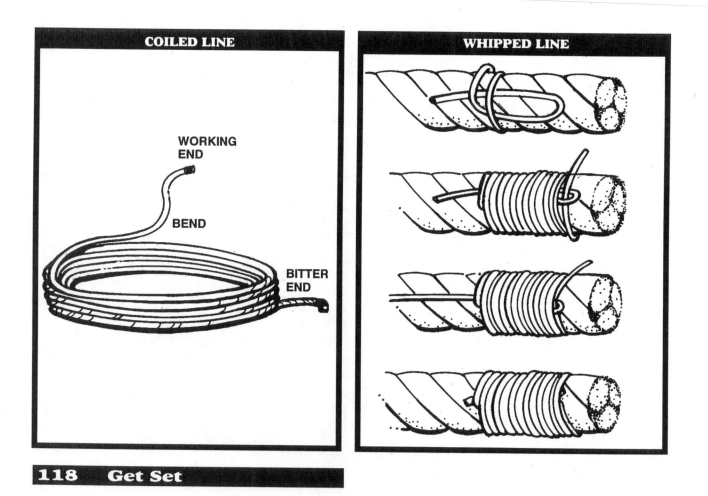

COILED LINE

WORKING END

BEND

BITTER END

WHIPPED LINE

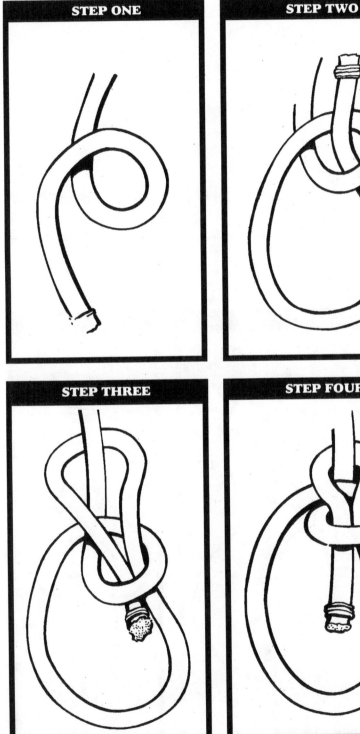

STEP ONE

STEP TWO

STEP THREE

STEP FOUR

SHEET BENDS, BIGHTS, AND BITTER ENDS

Bowline — the "King" of knots. It never slips, and no matter the amount of tension on the line, the knot can be untied easily and quickly. Uses for a bowline include tying a line to a sail, tying a painter line to the bow of the boat, or simply making a strong loop.

Figure Eight — a figure-eight knot is just one kind of bend. Use it to tie the bitter end of a line into a knot that won't slip through blocks or fair leads. A figure-eight knot can stop a line from unraveling.

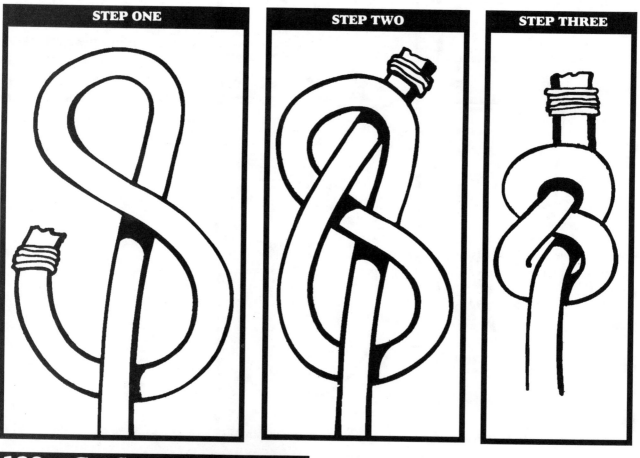

STEP ONE

STEP TWO

STEP THREE

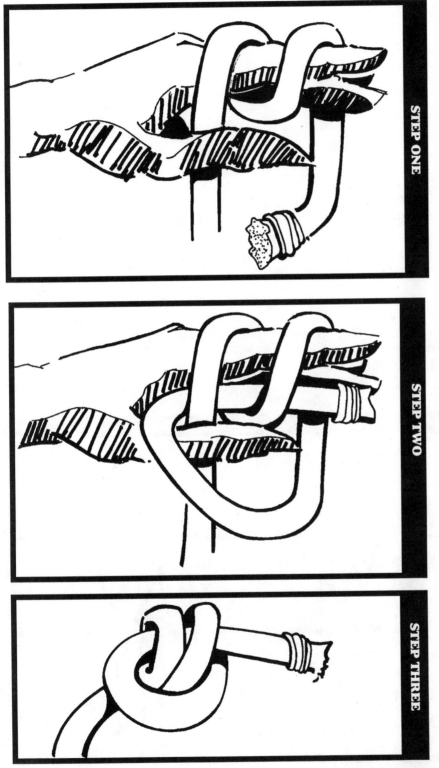

STEP ONE

STEP TWO

STEP THREE

Stopper Knot — this knot is a useful way to tie a line through the clew of a sail. Like a figure-eight knot, it can be used to stop a bitter end from slipping through a block. It is not so easy to untie as a figure-eight and lacks the holding power of a bowline.

K N O T S

Hitches — a hitch is another type of sheet bend. A half-hitch simply wraps the knot around an object. A fisherman's bend and a clove hitch are two half-hitches. Hitches are quick to tie and untie and are useful when docking, anchoring, or lashing a sail to the deck of the boat.

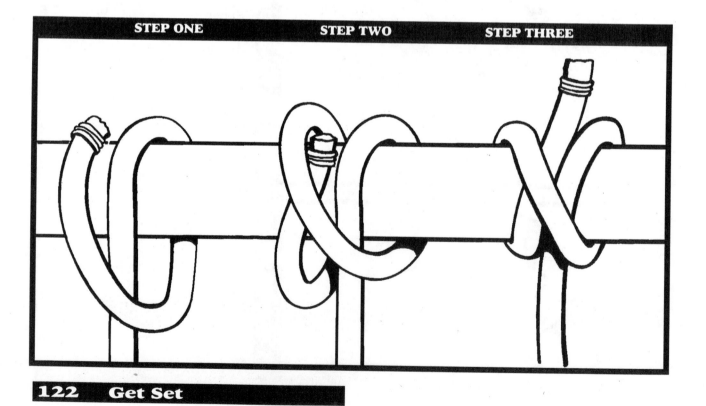

STEP ONE   STEP TWO   STEP THREE

K N O T S

Square Knot or Reef Knot — this knot is perfect for tying two equal-size lines together. Also, this knot is easy to tie and untie, especially when reefing the mainsail to the boom.

TYING A SQUARE KNOT

Sheet Bend — a sheet bend is like a square knot, but is used to tie two different objects together.

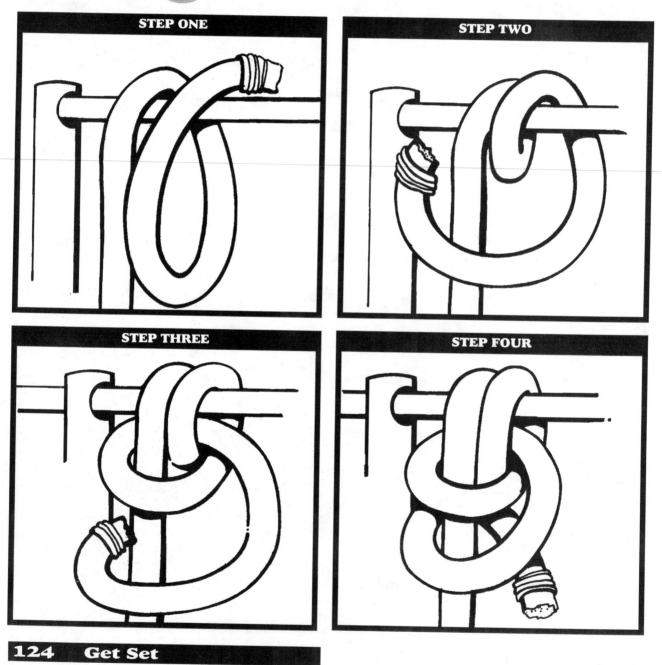

STEP ONE

STEP TWO

STEP THREE

STEP FOUR

HARDLY HARDWARE

▲ No matter the size of the boat, deck hardware makes sailing easy. Sailing used to require finding 20 or 30 large men to hoist the sails on the sleek old yachts. Now, by using a winch, a few blocks and the right fairleads to ease the pressure loads, only one or two people are needed to do the same task.

Even the small dingy has deck hardware — a cleat, a fairlead, or block. The larger the boat, the more the hardware.

Winches provide a mechanical advantage for a hoisting a sail or trimming it in. The most common kind of winch is called the drum winch. Depending upon the size of the boat, a drum winch can have up to three speeds or gears. This helps when the pressure load becomes too great.

Large boats, such as those that race in the Americas' Cup, use central winch handles, also known as "coffee grinders." Most conventional sailboats only need a single-handed or double-handed winch handle.

DOCKING

10

DOCK, DOCK, GOOSE

▲ Whether you're leaving the dock or returning home, the procedures to follow are important, especially with tides or currents. For safety reasons, be sure you know how to untie and retie the boat properly. First let's look at leaving the dock.

Departing is easy without too much wind, a large tide or a strong current. But if you have to deal with adverse conditions, know what you are up against and follow these steps:

When you are on the leeward side of the dock

- Cast off only the stern line.
- Point the bow into the wind.
- Hoist the sails, cast off the bowline and reverse the boat from the dock with either the sails, paddles, or engine.
- Once clear, trim the sails, and you are safely off!

Before you try this, practice with either an anchored float or a mooring buoy. If the boat can't point into the wind or you are on the windward side of the dock, you must push away from the dock first and then raise your sails into the wind when you are clear.

DOCKING

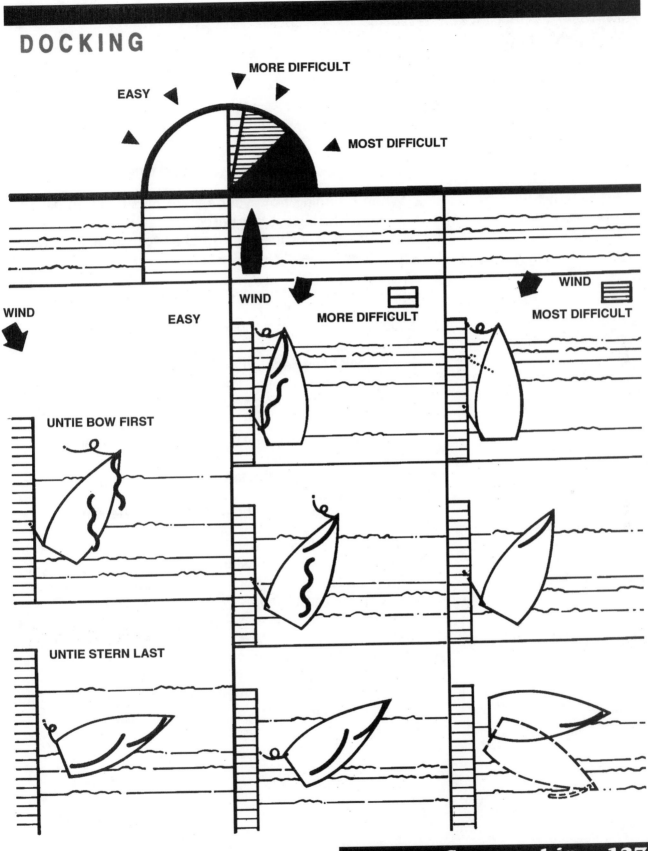

EASY

MORE DIFFICULT

MOST DIFFICULT

WIND

EASY

WIND

MORE DIFFICULT

WIND

MOST DIFFICULT

UNTIE BOW FIRST

UNTIE STERN LAST

DOCKING

10

HOMEWARD BOUND

▲ When returning from your sail, always have an escape route planned in case things get complicated. It is much better and safer for you and the boat to make two or three tries rather than to crash violently into the dock.

When docking on the leeward side of the dock

- Make your final approach into the wind or current.
- Be ready to fend off.
- Have dock lines secured and ready to use.
- With your bow pointed towards the dock and the boat gliding slowly, turn the boat parallel to the dock and secure the bow line.
- Secure the stern line — it is best if someone on the dock is there to catch the line.
- Going very slowly is the key to a safe landing.

When docking on the windward side of the dock

- Approach the dock from at least three boat lengths away.
- Lower the sails into the wind.
- Turn back toward the dock — if you have to slow down, make an "S" or "360" turn.
- Remember that the wind will push you — have an escape route in mind.
- With the boat gliding, turn the boat, bow first, parallel to the dock.
- Fend off with a fender, cushion or lifejacket — never use any part of your body!
- Secure dock lines.

DOCKING

Fenders protect a boat from the dock, pilings and other boats. Use a fender board when you have to dock a boat against an uneven surface.

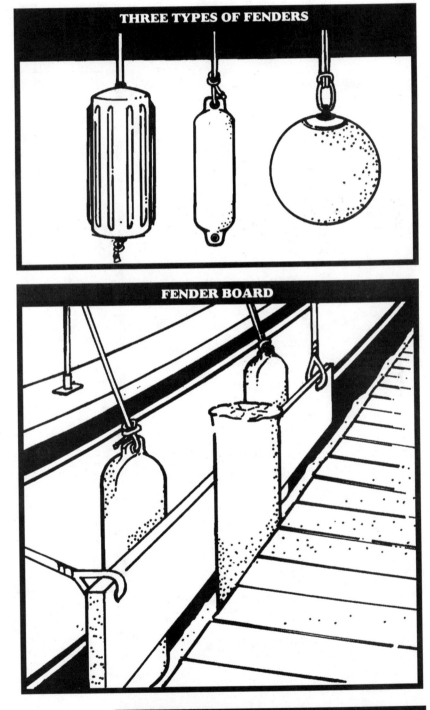

THREE TYPES OF FENDERS

FENDER BOARD

DOCKING

10

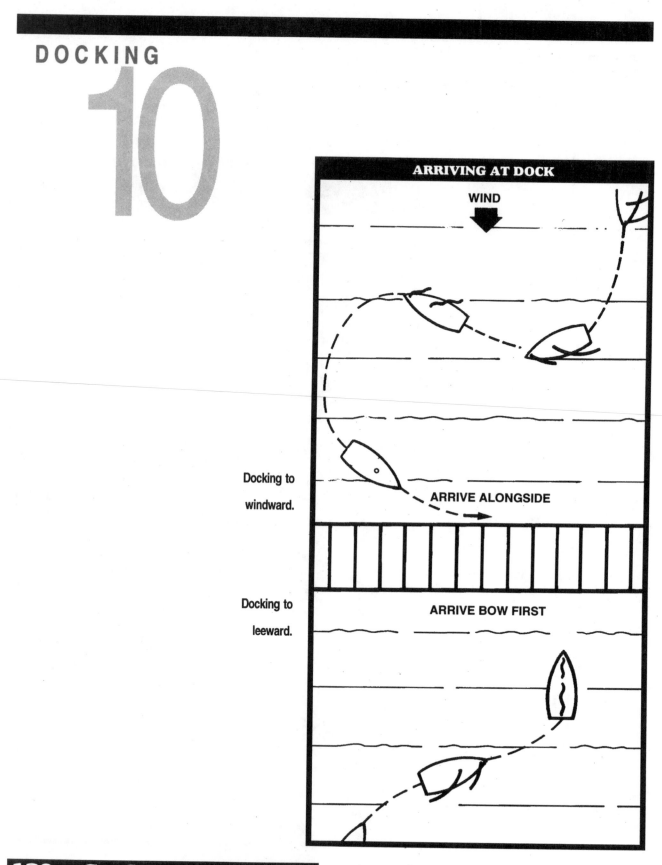

ARRIVING AT DOCK

WIND

Docking to
windward.

ARRIVE ALONGSIDE

Docking to
leeward.

ARRIVE BOW FIRST

ANCHORING

ANCHORS AWEIGH

▲ Knowing how to anchor your boat means you can secure your boat safely. You can enjoy the benefits of cruising, spending the night in a bay, being able to go ashore and explore, or just stopping for lunch.

Anchoring can also help in an emergency situation — such as when the weather is too rough or your engine has failed and you need to wait for help.

WHERE TO STOP

▲When choosing a place to anchor, remember that you need a place that is well sheltered from the wind and waves. The location should not be too shallow or too deep. When you anchor you must not be too close to other boats. All boats must swing freely, not getting tangled in each others' rode.

On most government charts, an anchor symbol (check the legend) will designate the best anchorages. Sometimes, a chart will show a "Harbor of Refuge," the best place to anchor in a storm.

ANCHORING

10

HOW TO ANCHOR
(WITHOUT A MOTOR)

1. Lower the jib, clear the forward area.

2. Know the depth.

3. Prepare the anchor — flake the line or chain and secure the anchorline to the boat. Hold the anchor outside the boat.

4. Head the boat into the wind, slowing almost to a stop.

5. Lower the anchor, being careful to not drop the anchor or throw it directly out of the boat.

6. Let out enough rode, generally three to seven times the water depth (high water in tidal areas).

7. Backwind the main briefly to make sure the anchor holds.

8. You are "lying at anchor" when your line is holding and the bow points into the wind.

* Be sure to continuously check that you are anchored — set up a watch system and use a landmark on shore to make sure that you don't drag.

* If you have a motor, the steps are generally the same except that you lower both the main and jib sails and, once you have enough rode out, slowly and carefully put the boat into reverse for two to five seconds to secure the anchor.

* To see how much scope has been let out, mark your anchor line every ten feet.

ANCHORING

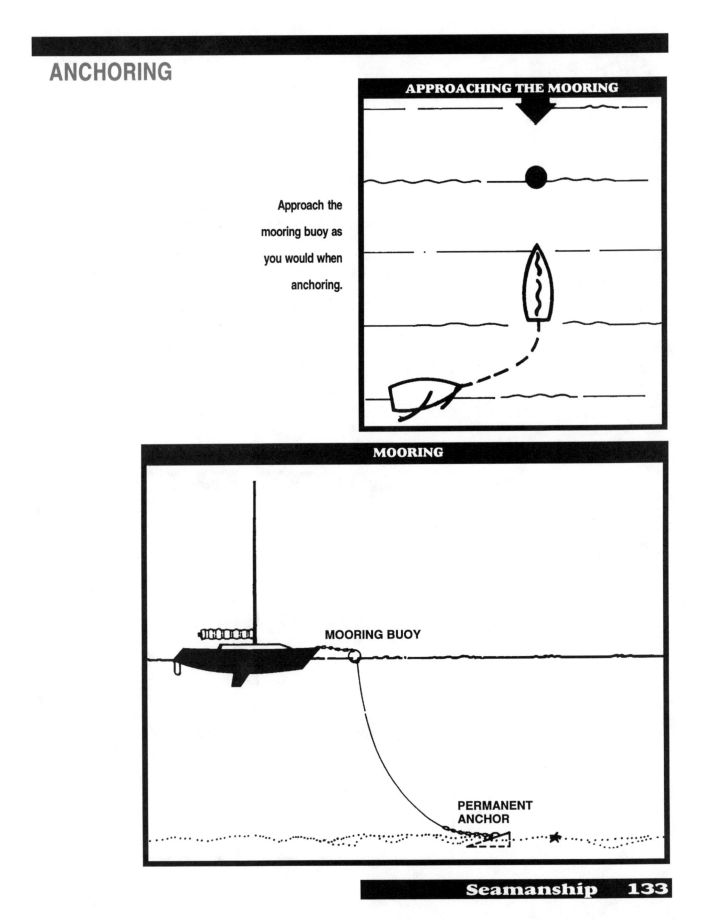

APPROACHING THE MOORING

Approach the mooring buoy as you would when anchoring.

MOORING

MOORING BUOY

PERMANENT ANCHOR

THE IDEAL SEABED
AND VARIOUS ANCHORS

▲ The bottom conditions help determine the correct anchor. Good seabeds are mud, sand, or clay. An area full of weeds, rocks, or coral can be tough to secure to or get away from. Look at your charts before you anchor to know the best anchorage. Never trust the anchor to hold — using a plow for weeds or sand, a danforth for soft mud, clay or sand, and a grapnel for coral or rocks will secure your boat the best.

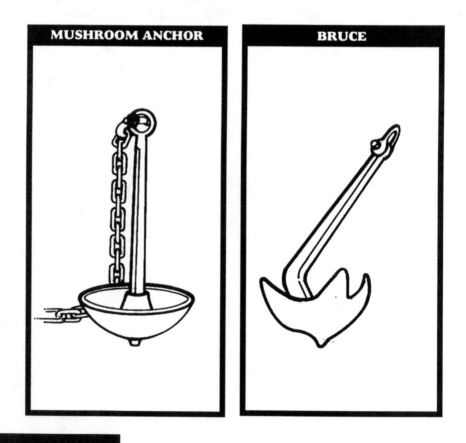

MUSHROOM ANCHOR

BRUCE

PULLING UP

▲ When leaving your anchorage, pull up the rode so the bow of the boat is almost directly over the anchor. Be sure not to run over the anchor. If the anchor is stuck, try pulling it up from a different angle. After the anchor is on deck, clean it off with a bucket of water. Never drag it through the water — this is a good way to fall overboard, lose the anchor or even put a hole in your boat.

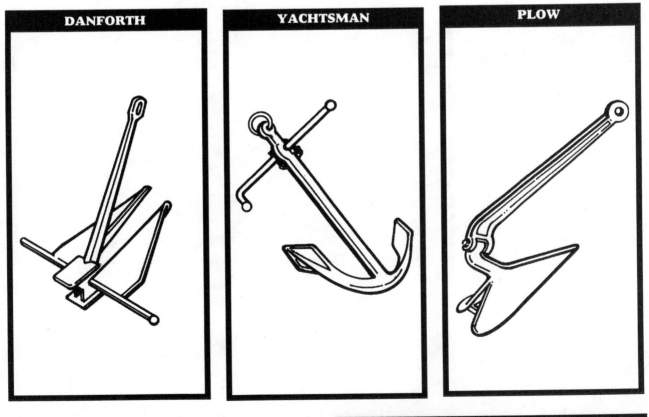

DANFORTH

YACHTSMAN

PLOW

STORMY SEAS

STORMY SEAS

▲ Storms are a common occurrence — the United States experiences more than 100,000 storms per year. Only one or two percent of these storms are considered violent. Yet every sailor must be ready for the occasional squall, thunderstorm or even gale-force wind.

Boats can usually handle violent seas or strong winds — sails and crew have a more difficult time during a storm, unless the crew is well prepared for any weather change.

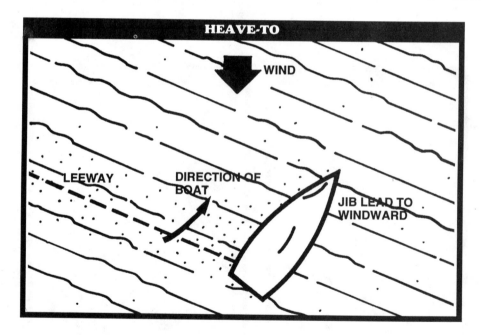

BEING PREPARED

- Preparing for a storm means many things:
- Knowing how to store all sailing gear properly.
- Knowing what the weather forecast is.
- Knowing how to dress using foul weather gear.
- Knowing how to reef the sails.
- Knowing how to heave - to.

Again, being prepared for rough weather makes the going easier. Avoid violent conditions. Take all safety precautions and, if needed, take shelter in a harbor of refuge or safe port. Make a distress call only when there is an emergency.

If you are sailing a dingy, being prepared means not sailing when the wind is too strong for the boat. Make sure that you never go out sailing without letting someone ashore know your plans. If an emergency occurs, never abandon ship and try to swim to shore.

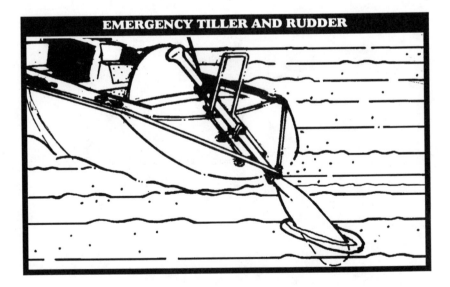

EMERGENCY TILLER AND RUDDER

KNOW YOUR NAVIGATION

▲ If you are planning a sail, check a chart. Charts are full of information on water depth, places of interest, good anchorages, and aids to navigation.

Knowing your navigation also means that you can use the various instruments, like parallel rules, a compass, a Loran or GPS, or even the complicated sextant. These instruments can determine where you are, how far you are from your destination, and your location in an emergency. Knowing the navigation rules is also important because of Coast Guard requirements such as using lights from sunset to sunrise and during reduced visibility, fog or storms.

Navigation is finding your way and includes pilotage, plotting a course, fixing a position, making a passage and following marks or buoys. Perfecting your navigating skills takes time, practice, and further study.

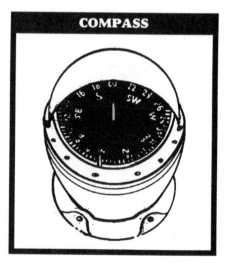

COMPASS

NAVIGATION

THE POLES

▲ The earth has a geomagnetic field due to a positive pole (the north pole) and a negative pole (the south pole). Although we use only the north pole to find a compass position, the Earth really has two magnetic poles.

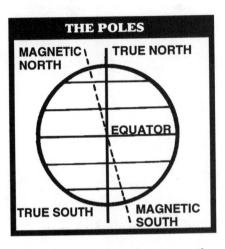

The magnetic north pole is not the true, geographic north —the magnetic north pole is south by southwest of true north. And, the magnetic north pole continues to move!

THE TOOLS TO USE

▲ The compass is the most important instrument used in navigation. Also, knowing your starting position, time of travel, speed of travel, and direction of travel gives you a position based on "dead reckoning."

Using an accurate chart, parallel rulers, dividers, a log book, a Loran-C or Global Position System, and a depth sounder gives a more accurate position.

Due to magnetic variation, magnetic deviation and any geographic change, charts and compasses must be updated frequently.

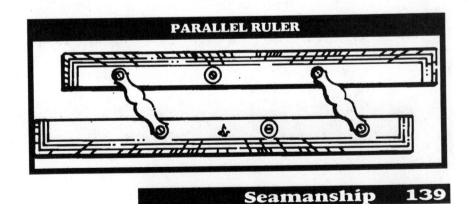

NAVIGATION

THE CHART

▲ A chart has a lot of useful information. Careful study of a chart will give you details on water depth, shipping lanes, hazards and tidal streams. Charts show buoys, light or sound patterns on aids for navigation, entrances to harbors and latitude and longitude lines. If a passage is potentially dangerous, the U.S. Coast Guard places range marks to make the passage safer. These are also well marked on a chart.

Charts come in many scales. Some charts are of the entire coastline, while some are of a specific area. Surveys are continuously taken to keep the charts fully updated.

Taking a navigational course will give you precise methods for navigating. And, you can explore exciting navigational techniques like celestial navigation, GPS and Loran-C plotting or planning.

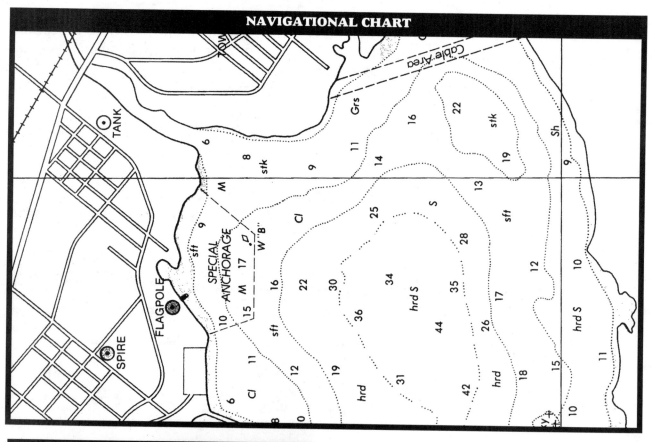

NAVIGATIONAL CHART

AIDS TO NAVIGATION

▲ Many internationally accepted standards are used in navigation. You are required to use bow, stern and steaming lights for passage from sunset to sunrise. All vessels must carry some sort of sound-producing device. Vessels longer than 26 feet must carry a whistle or bell. These are especially important to use when fog rolls in.

Buoys are designed with specific colors, shapes, numbers, sounds or lights for navigation.

An international code of signals uses alphabetical and numerical flags for visual signals.

AIDS TO NAVIGATION

PREVENTING EMERGENCIES

▲ The best way to prepare for an emergency situation is to prevent the emergency. Make sure the boat is seaworthy and has emergency gear aboard (such as a fire extinguisher and lifejackets). Know how to operate the VHF radio; know how to retrieve someone who has fallen overboard; and know how to plug a hole or patch a leak. Know the distress signals and how to jury rig a rudder or sail. Finally, have lights, whistles or a horn to attract attention and signal for help.

Accidents happen when you least expect them. Most fatalities are due to capsizing or falling overboard, most injuries are due to poor judgment and most collisions occur when the skipper is not paying attention to other boats, rocks or debris. Being tired, intoxicated or taking unnecessary risks greatly increases your chances for an accident.

Remember, "safe boating is no accident."

EMERGENCY SITUATIONS

▲ If an emergency occurs, follow these steps:

1. Evaluate the situation.
- Determine what is wrong.
- Do not panic, no matter how serious the situation.
- Decide who does what in the emergency.

2. Control the situation.
There are many situations that require immediate attention— a boat sinking, a person falling overboard, a capsize, etc. Do your best to control the situation. Get out the emergency gear. Never risk your life to save a life; use a life-saving device.

3. Call for help.
Use distress signals, both visual (flares, water dye, an orange flag) and audio (whistle, horn, radio).

4. Give first aid.

Many organizations give certified first aid and life-saving courses — take one every year.

Know CPR and know how to give standard first aid.

5. Prepare for help to arrive.

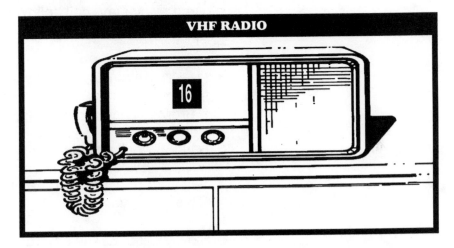

VHF RADIO

IF YOU HEAR A DISTRESS SIGNAL

1. Listen for a response by the Coast Guard or other emergency response agency.

2. If the message is not answered, answer the call by giving the distressed vessel's name, give your boat's name and call sign and tell them that you have received their distress call.

3. Listen for any response from the distressed vessel or from any of the other vessels in the area. Write down any information you can.

4. Offer the distressed vessel assistance and determine how you can best help.

5. Keep them informed of where you are, when you will arrive to help, and if you have contacted other assistance.

6. If you are not needed to help, stand by on the emergency channel until the situation has been cleared.

EMERGENCIES

10

MAY DAY, MAY DAY

▲ A "May Day" distress call means that life is in danger. If you place a "May Day" call, follow these steps:

1. Use the VHF radio on channel 16.

2. Say "May Day" three times.

3. Say your call signal three times. "WZH-9367."

4. Say your boat name three times.
   "This is the yacht _____ ."

5. Slowly describe the emergency. "Our boat is _____ and we have _____ people aboard."

6. Slowly give your location. "We are ____° latitude and we are ____° longitude." or "We are four miles due east from the nine-mile tower."

7. Tell what the boat looks like. "We are on a large white-hulled sailboat with a large blue graphic on the side."

8. Say the word "over" and wait a few seconds.

9. Stand by for replies.

If your situation is not life threatening, repeat the "May Day" procedure but use the word "Pan" instead. Placing a false distress call is against federal law and is punishable by large fines and possible imprisonment.

P F D

PUT YOUR PFD ON, PDQ

▲ How can you prevent 90 percent of the drownings that occur every year? Make everyone wear a PFD, or Personal Flotation Device. Most PFDs are comfortable and make you look like a pro. Also, be sure to care for your PFD:

- Don't use it for a boat fender.

- Don't put your PFD away wet.

- Don't dry your PFD on any heaters, dryers, or radiators — let it air dry!

- Don't forget to check your PFDs every year to make sure they still work.

PFDs are important to wear for two reasons:

1. They help you float in the water.

2. They keep you warm.

All states require PFDs on all vessels; the U.S. Coast Guard sets standards of how many PFDs and of what type should be aboard the boat.

THERE ARE FIVE TYPES OF PFD'S

Type I

(Off-Shore Life Jacket) — this PFD provides the most flotation. This PFD can turn an unconscious wearer face up. It is the easiest to put on and is easily visible from a long distance.

TYPE I

Type II

(Near-Shore Buoyant Vest) — this PFD is also designed to turn an unconscious wearer face up. It can be less bulky and more comfortable to wear than a Type I PFD. But it provides less flotation than the Type I PFD.

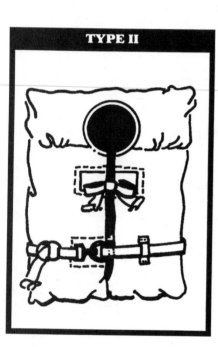

TYPE II

Type III

(Flotation Aid) — this PFD is comfortable and allows the most freedom of movement. But this PFD can't turn an unconscious wearer face up. Neither is this PFD made for survival in rough water.

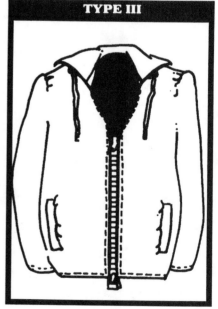

TYPE III

Type IV

(Throwable Device) — this PFD is meant to be thrown, not worn. It is not made for unconscious victims, children, or non-swimmers. Nor is this PFD meant for survival in rough water.

Type V

(Inflatable Device or a Special-Use Device) — these PFDs provide the least flotation. They are made for specific conditions or require manual inflation.

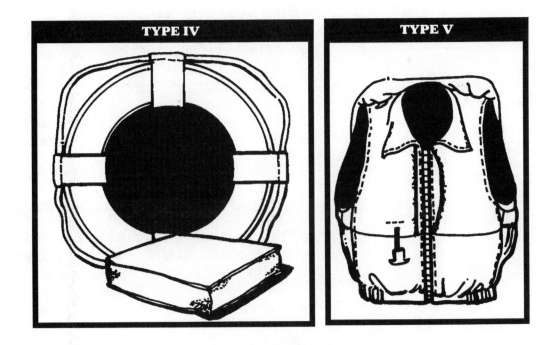

TYPE IV   TYPE V

SAFETY

10

THE SAFE BOAT

▲ Check your boat before each race or practice day. Make sure that all fittings are tight, nothing sharp is exposed. (An open ring ding may give you a boat bite — take precautions and tape your pins). Check your flotation tanks, as a capsize sometimes fills them up with water. Think of how slow you'll go or whether the boat will right itself if you capsize.

Once you have gone over the boat, make sure you have the following items on board:

- Enough PFDs
- Plenty of water and sunscreen
- Small first-aid kit (with Band-aids!)
- Extra pins, ring dings or fittings
- Tool kit with screw drivers, vise grips, tape
- Bailers
- Horn and whistles
- Flares and fire extinguishers

This list might not be enough. Plan ahead and prepare your own checklist to remember all the extras you might need.

DRESS FOR SAILING SUCCESS

▲ There are two things you need to consider before each sail — how hot it will be and how cold it will be. The best way to dress is in layers because you can always take something off.

What are the essentials?

- sunglasses
- gloves
- hat or visor

- foul - weather gear (wet suits/drysuits)
- Cold: long underwear, long pants, sweater, jacket, wool hat
- Hot: shorts, t-shirt

Clothing today is functional, and there are many outdoor companies that specialize in sailing gear. Just remember to find comfortable yet functional clothing.

BRR, IT'S COLD

▲ What happens when you get cold? Usually, overexposure to cold air temperatures or water temperatures causes hypothermia — a serious condition that, if not remedied, could be fatal.

Dress for all
conditions.

FIRST SIGNS OF HYPOTHERMIA

- Shivering
- Dizziness
- Numbness
- Confusion
- Weakness
- Impaired Judgment
- Impaired Vision
- Drowsiness

HYPOTHERMIA STAGES		
Stages	**Body Temp (approx.)**	**Other Symptoms**
I. Shivering	99° - 91° F	speaking is difficult
II. Apathy	90° - 86° F	lack of coordination
III. Unconscious	85° - 81° F	pulse and respiration slowed
IV. Decreased breathing & heartrate	80° - 78° F	erratic pulse
V. Death	Below 78° F	

These signs may appear when you sail in water that is 70° fahrenheit or colder, and when someone is not dressed properly. By the way, your body cools down 25 times faster in water than in the air.

Being on the water is usually colder than being ashore. So stay as warm and as dry as possible to prevent overexposure and hypothermia. Use foul weather gear before it rains.

WHAT TO DO IF YOU FALL IN THE WATER OR CAPSIZE

1. Don't try to swim to shore.

2. Be aware that swimming lowers your body temperature.

3. Try to get on top of the boat (a dry area) — the more your body is out of the water the warmer you will be.

4. Keep your head out of the water.

5. Use the H.E.L.P. (Heat Escape Lessening Procedure), or the huddle position to stay warm.

6. Know that smaller, thinner people need more warmth than larger people.

HYPOTHERMIA CHART		
Water Temperature	**Exhaustion Occurs In**	**Survival Time Is**
32.5° F	Under 15 minutes	15-45 minutes
32.5°- 40° F	15-30 minutes	30-90 minutes
40° - 50° F	30-60 minutes	1-3 hours
50° - 60° F	1-2 hours	1-6 hours
60° - 70° F	1-7 hours	2-40 hours
70° - 80° F	3-12 hours	3-indefinitely

10

IF YOU RESCUE SOMEONE WHO HAS BEEN OVEREXPOSED

1. Take the person to the driest and warmest area.

2. Remove wet clothing.

3. Apply heat — use a blanket, towel, body warmth (lie on top of the person), etc.

4. Give warm drinks — not alcohol or caffeine. Give warm water or broth.

5. Seek medical attention if:

   A. the person is violently shivering; or

   B. the skin is blue and the body is rigid.

HEAT EMERGENCIES

▲ Heat stress, heat stroke, and heat exhaustion are just as serious as hypothermia. A heat emergency is called hyperpyrexia. Drinking plenty of water, wearing light clothing, wearing a hat and sunglasses all help prevent heat emergencies.

The three types are:

Heat Stress — sluggishness, muscle spasms and muscle cramps are the first signs of overexposure to heat.

Heat Exhaustion — excessive sweating, headaches, nausea (dizziness and vomiting) and cool, moist skin are the next signs.

Heat Stroke — hot skin, very red face, plus the signs of stress and exhaustion top this stage. This stage is life threatening and requires immediate medical attention.

Overexposure to the sun or heat can easily be avoided. Most heat emergencies begin when a person does not drink enough water on hot, humid days with little breeze.

What To Do

1. Move the person to a cooler place.

2. Lay the person on his or her back and elevate the feet.

3. Cool the person with wet towels or blankets.

4. Contact EMS (Emergency Medical Services) if the person shows signs of heat exhaustion or heat stroke.

5. Be aware that the person may go into shock. Keep the person comfortable and lying down. Do not give liquids if the person seems to be in shock.

SAILING IS SAFE

▲ Sailing is a safe sport if you take precautions to prevent injuries and overexposure. Make sure that you are in physical shape to sail; eat right and exercise. Check the weather forecast for any signs of storms. Watch out for electrical power lines and make sure that you never go sailing without telling someone or having a safety boat out with you.

11
RACING

THE RACE COURSE

▲ Sailboat racing is an integral part of advanced sailing. Racing need not be an intense campaign to win — racing can be a fun and exciting way to sail with friends.

Racing improves sailing skills and furthers your understanding of what to do on the water. Review the sections on Rules and Tactics for an overall picture of racing.

THE START

▲ The sailing instructions and the skipper's meeting detail where the race course is located. You will get information on the starting sequence and the precise time of your start. Also, you will get information on what visual and audible signals to expect as you race.

A typical starting sequence of more than one class of boats may begin with a warning signal 10 minutes before the start for Class "A". A visual signal for the warning is a white shape; some sort of sound signal is given as the white shape is being raised.

At one minute before the five-minute signal, the warning signal is lowered.

Precisely five minutes before the start of the race for Class "A", you'll hear a preparatory signal — usually a blue flag and sound signal. This can also be the announcement of the beginning of the ten-minute sequence for Class "B".

One minute before the start, the blue shape is lowered. At the start, a red flag is raised with an accompanying sound signal. Once more, this would indicate that Class "A" starts the race and Class "B" has 5 minutes before its start.

11

ALL CLEAR

▲ Using the International Code Flags, race committees signal certain events. If the start needs to be postponed, the answering pennant is raised and usually two immediate sounds are heard.

Other signals the race committee can give are:

Individual Recall — when one boat starts earlier than the starting signal and needs to re-start the race.

General Recall — when too many boats are over the starting line before the starting signal. The entire class is recalled to start again.

Abandonment — when the race is called off to be re-sailed another time.

SAILING THE COURSE

▲ The race committee usually gives compass courses to the marks on the race course. Sometimes, the committee only gives one compass course with the understanding that the race course is an equilateral triangle or an isosceles triangle. Before the race, know these courses and have them written down on the boat.

Code flag "B" is the protest flag and must be displayed according to the sailing instructions. Use the protest flag anytime you believe an infraction of the rules has occurred.

Remember your tactical plan and pick sailing angles that seem to be the quickest and shortest distance to the marks. The race course is designed to test your skills while sailing at different points to the wind.

While racing, the race committee can use signals to note mark changes, a shortened course, life-jacket requirements or a canceled race. Always be aware of possible changes and know what the sailing instructions say to do in certain racing situations.

The finish of the race can be signalled or just noted. Again, the race committee will determine the procedure and will describe it in the sailing instructions.

READ MORE ABOUT IT

▲ Many books are devoted to racing skills — use the recommended reading list as a good source of information. Racing is truly a fun way to build your sailing skills and meet others that share a passion for the sport.

 **ATTITUDE**

COMMITTING TO WINNING

▲ Making a commitment to win is not the same as simply winning a race. Winning means being in shape to sail, taking care of your boat, always displaying good sportsmanship, practicing your skills, and respecting yourself, your crew, your competitors and your environment.

ATTITUDE IS EVERYTHING

▲ Psychological studies show that the most successful athletes have learned how to have a healthy mind and body. Mental training is a concept that is still being learned about. But, always having an upbeat, positive approach makes any situation easier to handle.

Physical training is a much more developed concept. Cross-training improves physical fitness and adds variety to work-outs. Your doctor or an exercise physiologist can suggest ways of staying in shape. They can also suggest a nutritional diet to keep your energy level high, your mental concentration at its most, and your well-being healthy.

Make winning a life-long commitment to yourself. Having a proper diet, getting regular exercise, and keeping a positive attitude are important aspects to areas other than sailing. The more routine you make these commitments, the easier the commitment to winning becomes.

13

JOURNAL

KEEPING A JOURNAL

▲ Writing down your experiences gives you a valuable record of many things: your performances; things you may want to change; what went right while racing; what not to do when things go wrong.

Having a float plan helps friends and relatives ashore know where you are, how many people are with you and an expected time of arrival. Also, a float plan is designed to help you in an emergency.

An operating check list gives you an idea of what to take out sailing, what not to leave at the dock and what to store away. And a tactical game plan is a quick way to make decisions. The following journal ideas have been used successfully, but they are just ideas and can be changed to suit your purposes.

Other journal ideas would be to record your sail trim, speed and the best place to lead the sail under the conditions. More great journal ideas include a tuning guide, maintenance chart or practice-session record.

Opposite: Hatch

Brown makes

notes at the MIT

Sailing Center in

Cambridge,

Massachusetts.

FLOAT PLAN

▲ Leave your float plan with a friend, a relative, marina operator or another sailor. Be sure to notify that person when you return so that the float plan can be discarded.

1. Description of boat

2. Number of persons on board

3. Radio equipment

4. Estimated time of arrival

5. Car parked at

6. I will call about my trip progress

7. If not at destination by

8. If emergency arises

OPERATING CHECKLIST

▲ Be sure to note any maintenance needs and continue adding to the list any important items not mentioned.

Sails, rudder, centerboard, spinnaker, pole, etc.

Navigational aids, charges, sailing instructions

Extra tools, maintenance equipment

Food and water

Proper clothing, hats, sunscreen, foul-weather gear

Life jackets, safety equipment

Paddles, oars, and bailers

Anchor and extra lines

Other _____

Other _____

Other _____

JOURNAL 13

TACTICAL PLAN

Weather Forecast:

Wind Strength:

Wave Height:

Temperature:

Clouds:

Current or Tide:

Any Current or Tide Changes:

Race Course Strategies:

Start Line:

Courses to Sail:

Opponents to Watch:

Favored Side of the Course:

Wind Shifts or Oscillations:

Courses to be Sailed:

SAILING EVALUATION

▲ This is a personal evaluation of your sailing performance. These are questions that can help you analyze your skills and decide if you are satisfied with your performance. They also help you determine how to improve.

On a scale of 1 to 10, how would you rate the day?

Could the day have gone better?

Were any mistakes made? Could these mistakes have been avoided? How?

What was the best part of the day? Could you repeat this?

Is there any sailing skill that you need to practice more? How could you practice and feel confident about mastering this sailing skill?

Did you follow your plans?

14

PROJECTS TO LEARN MORE

Many of the skills in "Get Ready, Get Set, GO!" can be learned in more fun ways than from a book. Here are hands-on ways to increase your knowledge.

The Weather — make your own forecast.

Tools needed

- barometer

- outdoor temperature thermometer

- camera

- paper, glue, and pens

Take pictures of the sky for a week. Record the barometer reading and air temperature for the particular sky condition each day. After the pictures are developed, make a photo album of your sky-watching events. Note barometer and thermometer readings. Can you make any predictions of future weather conditions? What happened when the barometer rose or fell? How did this effect the weather? Can you identify the different cloud patterns?

Atmospheric Pressure — understanding pressure.

Tools needed

- a plumber's plunger

- a smooth surface

Wet the plunger bottom. Push the plunger down on a smooth surface. Notice how the plunger sticks — see what happens when you push the plunger down on an uneven surface. Can you see how the outside air pressure is greater than the inside air pressure?

Opposite: Randy
Smythe shows
strategy at Low
Tide Yacht Club in
New Bedford,
Massachusetts.

The Rules — understanding them.

Tools needed

- two to four model sailboats

- playing board

- rule book

Pick a rule out of the rule book and role-play any infringement of the rule. Think of the scenario in which the rule is broken, how to have avoided the situation, and how to remedy it.

Sail Theory—understanding lift.

Tools needed

- a spoon

- a faucet with running water

Hold the spoon with your thumb and first finger. With the curved part of the spoon close to the running water, notice how the spoon gets sucked into the free-flowing water. As the spoon gets closer to the water the pressure differences lift the spoon up. What happens if you angle the spoon differently? Is the lift greater or is it reduced?

Sail Theory — pressure.

Tools needed

- a watermelon seed

Squeeze the seed equally until the seed is forced out of your thumb and first finger. Try this with more pressure from only one finger. This shows how two pressures together equal a forward movement. The more equal the pressure, the further forward the seed will go.

PROJECTS

Sail Theory—Flotation.

Tools needed

- large bucket

- different objects:

  a pencil, coins, paper clip, a piece of wood

Put the objects in the bucket and notice which ones float. Why would one object float and one sink?

Tactics and Wind Shifts — who's ahead.

Tools needed

- graph paper

- ruler

- pens

- objects that can show the wind and at least two boats

On the graph paper, draw a starting line, a windward mark and "ladder lines." Shift the wind and see which boat would be on the new "ladder" rung. Note: the ladder rung always shifts to a position perpendicular to the direction of the wind. What is the difference between a windshift while close-hauled and a windshift while running?

TEST YOURSELF

▲ Take this test to review what you've learned. Answers follow the test.

Weather
1. The wind is a result of:
   A. atmospheric pressure, radiation, and humidity
   B. an air mass
   C. a thunderstorm
   D. the jet stream

2. _____ clouds are thunderclouds.
   A. Cirrostratus
   B. Altocumulus
   C. Stratus
   D. Cumulonimbus

3. The most common type of fog found at sea is:
   A. smog
   B. radiation
   C. advection
   D. steam

Tides
4. Tides and currents are the same water movements.
   A. True, because they both move vertically.
   B. False, because currents only move horizontally.
   C. True, because they only occur during the full moon.
   D. False, because they only occur in rivers.

Sail Theory
5. The _____ force pulls the boat along.
   A. strong
   B. resultant
   C. lift
   D. velocity

6. Friction comes in two forms:
   A. skin and form
   B. horizontal and vertical
   C. Center of Effort and Center of Lateral Resistance
   D. lift and drag

Tuning & Rigging

7. The Center of Effort and Center of Lateral Resistance are equal, yet opposite forces.
   A. True, because of Newton's Law of Equilibrium.
   B. True, because of Bernouli's Law of Balance.
   C. False, because opposite forces are not equal.
   D. False, because twist moves the Center of Effort.

8. Weather helm is:
   A. when the boat capsizes
   B. when the boat has leeway
   C. when the boat wants to point into the wind
   D. when it rains

9. The running backstay controls:
   A. fore and aft bend of the mast
   B. the running engine
   C. a dead-down run
   D. the Center of Lateral Resistance

10. To reduce weather helm:
    A. trim the mast
    B. ease the mainsheet
    C. move the jib draft aft
    D. increase lift

The Rules

11. In the Racing Rules, a tack is completed when:
    A. the boat is tacking
    B. the boat is mast abeam
    C. the boat is not tacking or gybing
    D. the boat is gybing to windward

12. A stand-on vessel:
   A. can't move from its position
   B. is sailing
   C. is in a dangerous place
   D. has the right-of-way

13. Alcohol does not influence a skipper's ability to operate a sailboat safely.
   A. True, only drugs influence decisions.
   B. False, alcohol and drugs both impair the skipper's ability.
   C. True, the skipper is always in charge.
   D. False, only drugs influence decisions.

14. A sailboat always has the right-of-way except:
   A. when a motorboat is present
   B. when the boat is sailing
   C. when a freighter is navigating a channel
   D. when the sailboat is moving slowly

Skippering & Crewing

15. When a skipper says "ready about," the skipper is simultaneously tacking the boat.
   A. True, because "about" means "turn now."
   B. False, because the skipper is asking if the crew is ready to tack.
   C. True, because the skipper needs to do everything as fast as possible.
   D. False, because "about" means ease the jib about to the shrouds.

16. Communication means that the skipper does all the talking on the boat.
   A. False, the crew needs to give the skipper input.
   B. True, the skipper is in charge.
   C. False, only at mark roundings does the skipper give commands.
   D. True, the crew does not know enough sailing information to comment on.

Sail Trim

17. Mainsail draft is important to have because:
    A. it shows if the sail is trimmed properly
    B. it shows the camber of the sail
    C. it shows the Center of Effort and if the Center of Effort is in the proper place
    D. all of the above

18. An airbrake means:
    A. the sail is not stopping the wind
    B. the slot is applied
    C. the sail is not trimmed properly
    D. the telltales are breaking evenly

19. Spinnakers should be used:
    A. when only sailing a beat
    B. when the wind is not very strong
    C. when sailing a beam reach to a downwind course
    D. when the wind is 45 degrees to the bow

20. Surfing and planing are the same.
    A. False
    B. True
    C. Only when you sail off a beach
    D. Only when you sail off a dock

Tactics

21. Tactics are only used when racing.
    A. False
    B. True
    C. False, only when you sail on a keel boat
    D. True, only when you sail on a keel boat

22. A start on the favored end means:
    A. starting on the end closest to the windward mark
    B. starting on the lift tack
    C. starting on the knocked tack
    D. starting with clear air

23. The rhumbline and layline are always the same.
    A. True
    B. False
    C. Only true after a bad start
    D. Only true after barging

24. Downwind tack is also called gybing.
    A. True
    B. False
    C. Only true when sailing upwind
    D. Only true when sailing close hauled

25. Common tactical mistakes are:
    A. tacking too much
    B. having a poor attitude
    C. taking too many risks
    D. all of the above

Seamanship
26. Seamanship means knowing about:
    A. tying knots
    B. docking the boat
    C. knowing what to do in emergencies
    D. all of the above

27. A bowline knot should only be used on the bow of the boat.
    A. True
    B. False
    C. True, only when used on the anchor line
    D. True, only when used to rescue someone

28. The best place to dock is:
    A. on the windward side of the dock
    B. on the leeward side of the dock
    C. where you have an escape route planned for either A or B
    D. all of the above

29. Use the words "May Day" when calling in an emergency.
    A. True
    B. False
    C. True, when the emergency is life threatening
    D. True, when the emergency is not life threatening

30. A Type IV, throwable device, is okay to wear
    A. True
    B. False

31. A PFD should be thrown to someone who has fallen overboard.
    A. True
    B. False

32. Hypothermia and Hyperpyrexia are serious emergency conditions.
    A. True
    B. False

Navigation
33. Navigational buoys are good places to moor since they show deep water and anchorages.
    A. True
    B. False

34. Only large boats need to use lights at night.
    A. True
    B. False

GO!
35. Committing to winning means:
    A. having a positive attitude
    B. being physically fit
    C. conducting yourself in a sportsmanlike manner
    D. all of the above

36. The race course is:
    A. a place to improve sailing skills
    B. only for those who can win the race
    C. a place to take sailing seriously
    D. only for professionals

37. Code flags are visual signals on the race committee boat telling racing sail boats what to do.
    A. True
    B. False

ANSWERS

Answers

1. A	11. C	21. A	31. A
2. D	12. D	22. A	32. A
3. C	13. B	23. B	33. B
4. B	14. C	24. A	34. B
5. B	15. B	25. D	35. D
6. A	16. A	26. D	36. A
7. A	17. D	27. B	37. A
8. C	18. C	28. D	
9. A	19. C	29. C	
10. B	20. A	30. B	

RECOMMENDED READING

There are many books on sailing; most are dedicated to specific topics. Visit your local library, bookstore or ship's chandlery to find these great resources.

MAGAZINES

Sail (100 First Avenue, Charlestown, MA)

Sailing World (5 John Clarke Road, Newport, RI)

BOOKS

Sports Illustrated Small Boat Sailing — A Complete Guide, by David and Brad Dellenbaugh (New York: Time, Inc., 1990)

Start Sailing Right!, by Derrick Fries, 2nd ed. (U.S. Sailing Association, 1992)

The Complete Sailing Handbook, by Roland Denk (Munich: BLV Verlagsgesellschaft M6H, 1976)

Weather for Great Lakes Sailors, by John McMurray and Mal Sillars (1980)

The Handbook of Sailing, by Bob Bond, 5th ed. (London: Dorling Kindersley Ltd., 1980)

The Racing Edge, by Ted Turner and Gary Jobson (New York: Rutledge Books, Inc., 1979)

Tactics, by Rodney Pattisson (Great Britain: Fernhurst Books, 1983)

Dingy Helming, by Lawrie Smith (Camden, Maine: International Marine Publishing, 1986)

Tuning Yachts & Small Keelboats, by Lawrie Smith (Great Britain: Fernhurst Books, 1988)

Understanding the New Sailing Technology, by Sven Donalson (New York: Putnam 1990)

Looking at Sails, by Dick Kenny, 2nd ed. (Camden,Maine: International Marine Publishing, 1988)

Advanced Sailing Skills, by Don Griffin (Canada: Canadian Yachting Association, 1979)

B O O K S

Advanced Sailing, by Tony Gibbs (New York: St. Martin's Press, 1975)

1993-96 International Yacht Racing Rules (U.S. Sailing, 1993)

Time-Life Library of Boating (New York: Time-Life Books, 1976)

Advanced Racing Tactics, by Stuart Walker (New York: W.W. Norton, 1976)

World Cruising Routes, by Jimmy Cornell (Massachusetts: International Marine Publishing, 1990)

Cruising Boat Sailing, by Bob Bond and Steve Slight (New York: Alfred A. Knopf, 1983)

Hand, Reef & Steer, A Practical Handbook on Sailing, by Richard Henderson (Chicago: Contemporary Books, 1991)

Spacious Skies, by Richard Scorer and Argen Vevcaih (London: David & Charles Newton Publishing, 1989)

The New Glenans Sailing Manual, by James MacGibbon and Stanley Caldwell (Boston: R&R Donnelley & Sons Co., 1978)

McGraw-Hill Encyclopedia of Ocean and Atmospheric Sciences, Sybil P. Parker, Editor-in-Chief (New York: McGraw-Hill, Inc.)

GLOSSARY

ABANDONMENT   An abandoned race is one that is declared void at any time and that may be re-sailed.

ABEAM   A point or the middle of the boat that forms a 90° angle with the center line running from the bow to the stern.

AERODYNAMICS   The physical force of the air.

AIR MASS   A body of air that has the same pressure, temperature, and amount of moisture throughout the mass. It can be stable or unstable, tropical (warm), polar (cold), continental (over land), or maritime (over water) depending upon the origination of the air mass.

AIRFOIL   A foil designed to create lift when air flow hits it.

AMIDSHIP   The center or middle of the boat.

ANCHOR   Anything that secures a boat to the bottom.

ANCHORAGE   A specific place that is good for anchoring and is usually noted on charts.

ANEMOMETER   An instrument used to measure windspeed.

APPARENT WIND   The direction and/or speed of the wind measured in a moving boat. Apparent wind appears to be coming from a direction more forward than the true wind, because it is a result of true wind plus the movement of the boat.

ATMOSPHERIC PRESSURE   The weight of a column of air.

BABY STAY   A wire that supports the aft pull of the mast.

BACK/BACKING   Using the sail in an opposing direction so that the boat can heave-to, move backwards or help turn the boat.

BACKSTAY   A wire that supports the forward pull of the mast.

BARBERHAUL   A line attached to the jib to move the jib lead inboard or outboard.

BARGING   When starting, a boat approaches the windward starting area from a windward position outside the starting area.

GLOSSARY

BAROMETER An instrument that measures atmospheric pressure.

BATTEN A thin stiff object used to keep the leech of a sail supported.

BEAM The width of the boat.

BEARING AWAY Altering course away from the wind until a yacht begins to gybe.

BEARING The compass course of an object, from the boat or buoy.

BEATING Sailing to windward and close hauled.

BLANKET OR BAD AIR The disturbed airflow due to a wind shadow either from other boats, an island or obstruction.

BROACH While reaching or running, the boat rounds up toward the wind.

BROAD REACH Sailing downwind at approximately 135° away from the wind.

BUOY A floating mark to indicate a waterway entrance, a shoal, or other aid to navigation.

CAMBER The curved shape showing the fullness of a sail.

CENTER LINE An imaginary line drawn down the middle of the boat from the bow to stern.

CENTER OF EFFORT (CE) A point on a sail where the resulting aerodynamic forces meet to create lift.

CENTER OF EFFORT The exact position of the wind on the sails.

CENTER OF LATERAL RESISTANCE (CLR) A point on the centerboard or keel where the resulting hydrodynamicforces meet to aid in the lifting force on the boat.

CHAINPLATES Metal plates affixed to the hull that help take the weight or pressure load off the shrouds.

CHART A map of a body of water.

CHORD An imaginary line connecting the entry and exit areas of a sail, showing the amount of fullness. The chord is parallel of the foot of the sail.

GLOSSARY

CHUTE
A spinnaker.

CLOSE-HAULED
A yacht is close-hauled when sailing by the wind as close as she can lie with advantage in working to windward.

CLEAR AIR
The undisturbed airflow.

CLOSE-REACH
Sailing between 50° - 80° off the direction of the wind.

CLOUDS
The cooling of air produces water droplets that form into clouds.

CONCAVE
The inward curve of an object.

CONVEX
The outward curve of an object.

COVER
Watching the competition while trying to keep your boat between the mark and the competition.

COURSE
Sailing in a specific direction.

CURRENT
The horizontal, or sideways, flow of water.

DANGER ZONE
An arc of 112° degrees measured from dead ahead to off the starboard beam.

DEAD RECKONING
A method of navigation that uses compass course, boat speed and time travelled to determine a boat's position.

DISTURBED AIR/WATER
The term for wind or water that has not rejoined the free flowing air or water stream.

DIURNAL
One high tide and one low tide per day.

DOWNHAUL
A line attached to the spinnaker pole to keep the spinnaker pole from angling up and keeping the pole stable.

DRAFT
The convex area of a sail, usually referred to as camber.

DRAG[1]
After anchoring, the anchor does not hold, causing the boat to drift.

DRAG[2]
The force that resists the motion of an object.

GLOSSARY

EBB CURRENT	An outward flow of the water.
ENTRY	The curve of the leading edge (the part that the wind hits first) of a sail.
EXIT	The leech area, where the wind leaves the sail.
FAIRLEAD	A ring, eye, block or other device used to guide a line in a specific direction.
FALLING OFF	Going away from the wind.
FAVORED	An end of the starting or finishing line that is closer to windward mark, or to your boat respective of starting or finishing.
FETCH	Sailing a windward course that is not quite close hauled.
FINISHING	A yacht finishes when any part of her hull, or of her crew or equipment in normal position, crosses the finishing line in the direction of the course from the last mark, after fulfilling any penalty obligations under rule 52.2(b).
FIX	Finding the boat's position.
FLOOD CURRENT	An inward flow of the water.
FOG	Low-level clouds that contain a lot of moisture. Fog occurs as warm air hits a cool surface.
FOIL	The shape of certain objects designed to produce the most amount of lift with the least amount of drag.
FORCE	Pressure against an object resulting in a push or pull.
FORCE VECTOR	A line showing the direction in which the force is going.
FORM FRICTION	Friction that occurs when the airfoils or hydrofoils are not designed properly.
FREEBOARD	The part of the boat that is above the water.
FRICTION	Resistance against an object.
FRONT	The border between a warm air mass and a cool air mass.

GLOSSARY

FULLNESS	The depth, belly, or sag in the sail.
GIVE-WAY (BURDENED) VESSEL	The vessel which must keep clear of the privileged vessel.
GUY	A line attached to the spinnaker that controls the fore and aft position of the spinnaker pole.
GYBE/GYBING	A yacht begins to gybe at the moment when, with the wind aft, the foot of her mainsail crosses her center line, and completes the gybe when the mainsail has filled on the other tack.
HARBOR OF REFUGE	A harbor or port that is the safest place to anchor during a storm.
HEADING	The direction in which the boat is going according to the compass course.
HEAVE-TO	Backing the sails so that the boat makes little or no movement.
HEEL	When the force of the wind or water acts on a boat, it causes the boat to angle or incline.
HIGH PRESSURE	When cool, dry air sinks and the barometric pressure increases.
HIGH TIDE	When the flood current brings the water in and the water is at the highest level.
HUMIDITY	The amount of water the air can hold before becoming saturated.
HYDROFOIL	A foil designed to create lift in the water. This lift is also termed lateral resistance.
HYDRODYNAMICS	The physical force of the water.
IRONS	Pointing directly into the wind and not moving.
JET STREAM	A "river" of air that circles the Earth at 35,000 feet above sea level.
JIBE	See gybe.

GLOSSARY

JURY RIG	Using equipment to replace a damage boat part to keep the boat sailing.
KNOCK	A change in the boat's course, when the wind shifts, causing the boat to go away from the new wind.
KNOCKED	As the wind shifts or oscillates, the boat sails away from the previous course.
LAYLINE	An imaginary line showing the port and starboard course boundaries.
LEE BOW	A wind shadow effect that occurs when a leeward boat disturbs the airflow of a windward boat.
LEE HELM	What happens when the boat points away from the wind when you let go of the helm.
LEEWARD AND WINDWARD	The leeward side of a yacht is that on which she is, or, when head to wind, was, carrying her mainsail. The opposite side is the windward side. When neither of two yachts on the same tack is clear astern, the one on the leeward side of the other is the leeward yacht. The other is the windward yacht.
LEEWAY	The sideways movement of the boat due to a tide or current.
LEECH	The back or aft portion of a sail.
LIFT	There are two types of lift: 1) a change in the boat's course, when the wind shifts, causing the boat to head toward the new wind, and 2) the other type results from the high and low air pressures acting on an object, causing it to move in a resulting direction.
LIGHTNING	An electric charge.
LOW PRESSURE	When warm, moist air rises and the barometric pressure decreases.
LOW TIDE	When the ebb current takes the water out and the water level is at its lowest.
LUFF	The front portion of a sail.
LUFFING	Altering course towards the wind. Also, when a sail is fluttering.

GLOSSARY

LYING AT ANCHOR

When the anchor holds.

MAGNETIC DEVIATION

The compass difference between the boat's magnetic field and the earth's magnetic field. A boat's compass can be "swung" to eliminate this deviation.

MAGNETIC VARIATION

The difference between the true north pole or south pole and the magnetic north pole or south pole.

MARK

A mark is any object specified in the sailing instructions that a yacht must round or pass on a required side. Ground tackle and any object accidentally or temporarily attached to the mark are not part of it.

MAST ABEAM

A windward yacht sailing no higher than a leeward yacht is mast abeam when her helmsman's line of sight abeam from his normal station is forward of the leeward yacht's mainmast. A windward yacht sailing higher than a leeward yacht is mast abeam when her helmsman's line of sight abeam from his normal station would be, if she were sailing no higher, forward of the leeward yacht's mainmast.

MAST RAKE

The amount of tension of the backstay with the sails raised.

MOORING

A permament anchor.

MOTORBOAT

Any vessel propelled by machinery, including any sailing vessel under sail or power.

NAUTICAL MILE

A unit of measure in the air and at sea. Distance is based on the curvature of the Earth's surface. Also known as a knot.

NEAP TIDE

The smallest difference in tidal range that occurs during the first quarter and last quarter of the moon phases.

NEUTRAL HELM

When the boat continues straight when you let go of the helm.

GLOSSARY

OBSTRUCTION
An obstruction is any object, including a vessel under way, large enough to require a yacht, when more than one overall length away from it, to make a substantial alteration of course to pass on one side or the other, or any object that can be passed on one side only, including a buoy when the yacht in question cannot safely pass between it and the shoal or the object that it marks. The sailing instructions may prescribe that a specified area shall rank as an obstruction.

OFFSHORE
Going away from shore.

ONSHORE
Going toward the shore.

OSCILLATION
A "temporary" change in the wind direction.

OVERSTOOD
Sailing beyond the layline.

PINCHING
Sailing too close to the wind.

PLANE
When the lifting force of the boat, usually when on a reach, supports the boat so that the boat sails on top of the water, not through the water.

PLOT
A mark on a chart showing the boat's position.

POINT
The ability to get closer to the wind.

POLAR DIAGRAM
A series of calculations that determine target speeds for various wind speeds.

POSITION
A latitude parallel and a longitude meridian pinpointing a specific location. Both latitude and longitude are measured in degrees (°), minutes ('), and seconds or tenths of minutes.

POSTPONEMENT
A postponed race is one that is not started at its scheduled time and that can be sailed at any time the race committee may decide.

PRE-BEND
When the mast is bent backwards without the sails raised.

PREVAILING WESTERLIES
The direction of the wind, from west to east, that predominates in the Western Hemisphere.

PROLONGED BLAST
(ON WHISTLE) A blast of four to six seconds in duration.

GLOSSARY

PROPER COURSE

A proper course is any course that a yacht might sail after the starting signal, in the absence of the other yachts affected, to finish as quickly as possible. There is no proper course before the starting signal.

PROTEST

An action taken by a yacht, race committee or protest committee to initiate a hearing on a possible infringement of a rule or a consideration of redress in accordance with rule 68, 69, or 70.

QUARTER

A point on the boat between the beam and stern.

RACING

A yacht is racing from her preparatory signal until she has either finished and cleared the finishing line and finishing marks or retired, or until the race has been postponed or abandoned, or a general recall has been signalled.

RADIATION

The heating of the Earth by the sun.

RANGE

A fixed landmark used for exact steering.

REACH

Sailing with the wind on the beam of the boat.

REEF

Reducing the amount of sail being used.

RESULTANT FORCE

The total force created when lift and drag are combined.

RHUMBLINE

An imaginary line showing the direct course to the mark.

RIG TENSION

The amount of pressure on the shrouds.

RIG

The mast and fittings that hold the mast up.

RIGGING

Preparing the boat to sail and/or preparing the mast and shrouds to sail.

RIGHT-OF-WAY

The right and duty to maintain course and speed.

RODE

The total amount of anchor line used.

ROOM

Room is the space needed by a yacht to maneuver in a seamanlike manner in the prevailing conditions.

RUN

Sailing down wind.

GLOSSARY

RUNNING RIGGING — Rigging used for sail controls such as halyards and sheets.

RUNNING/BACK STAYS — Control the head stay tension.

SAILING — A yacht is sailing when using only the wind and water to increase, maintain or decrease her speed, with her crew adjusting the trim of sails and hull and performing other acts of seamanship.

SAILING VESSEL — Any vessel which is under sail alone, including any power vessel under sail alone.

SCOPE — The amount of anchor line used when anchoring. The ratio is usually 7 feet of anchor line per foot of water depth, but can change to 3 to 1 or even 10 to 1 depending upon conditions.

SEMI-DIURNAL — Two high tides and two low tides per day.

SHEET — The lines or rope used to control the sail.

SHORT BLAST (ON WHISTLE) — A blast of one to two seconds in duration.

SHROUD (SIDESTAY) — The side guide wires holding up the mast.

SKIN FRICTION — Friction that occurs under water and is caused by items such as a dirty boat bottom, poor paint job, or too large of a propeller.

SLACK TIDE — The time in between tides when there is no current.

SLOT — The vertical area between the main and the jib.

SPILL AIR — Not trimming the sail fully.

SPIN SHEET — A line attached to the spinnaker that controls the trim of the spinnaker.

SPREADERS — Struts (metal pieces) attached to the mast to keep the mast from bending improperly from the pushing or pulling of the shroud.

SPRING TIDE — The highest of high tides or the lowest of low tides that occurs during the new and full moon phases.

SQUALL — A fast-moving line of cold air that meets warm air. It usually results in a sudden thunderstorm that lasts between five and twenty minutes.

GLOSSARY

SQUARE — A term referring to a starting line or finish line that does not have a favored end.

STAGNATION POINT — The point where the velocity, or speed, is zero.

STALL — When an increase in drag and a decrease in lift stops the smooth flow on a foil or sail.

STALLING — The point on the foil where the airflow or waterflow is too disturbed (keeping the foil from working properly).

STAND-ON (PRIVILEGED) VESSEL — The vessel which has the right-of-way.

STANDING RIGGING — The mast supports' permanent fixtures like shrouds, spreaders and turn buckles.

STARTING — A yacht starts when, after fulfilling her penalty obligations, if any, under rule 51.1(c), and after her starting signal, any part of her hull, crew or equipment first crosses the starting line in the direction of the course to the first mark.

SURFING — Like planing except that the boat is moving down a wave.

SWING — While lying at anchor, the boat pivots around the anchor.

TACKING — A yacht is tacking from the moment she is beyond head to wind until she has borne away to a close-hauled course.

TARGET SPEED — The maximum boat speed.

TELLTALES — Yarn or strings attached to the sail showing the airflow.

TIDAL RANGE — The difference between high and low tides.

TIDE TABLES — The table that predicts when the high, low or slack tides will occur daily.

TIDE — The vertical, or up and down, water flow from the gravitational pull between the Earth and the moon.

TOPPING LIFT — A line attached to the spinnaker pole that raises and lowers the pole.

GLOSSARY

TRUE WIND The wind felt while not moving.

TUNING Fine adjustments made to the mast and sails to balance the boat and make it sail better.

TURNBUCKLES A fitting that allows the shroud to be attached to the boat with opposite threads on each piece so that they can be tightened without turning the shroud.

TWIST When the upper and lower portions of the sails are trimmed at different angles to each other, noticed when looking from the bottom to the top of the sail.

UNDERWAY Not at anchor, aground, or made fast to the shore.

VELOCITY MADE GOOD (VMG) A calculation showing the angular relationship between the boat, the true wind and the apparent sailing direction.

VESSEL Every description of watercraft used or capable of being used as a means of transportation on the water.

VISIBLE (When applied to lights) visible on a dark, clear night.

WEATHER To windward on the boat.

WEATHER HELM When the boat will point into the wind when you let go of the tiller or wheel.

WEIGHING ANCHOR Leaving the anchorage.

WIND SHIFT A "permanent" change in the wind direction.

WINDWARD see leeward and windward.

INDEX

Author
Julee Roth

Illustrators
Tong Sun-Suh
& Others

Editors
Carolyn Hines
Suzanne Lipshaw

Typist
Ryan

Designers
Lisa Gottlieb
Robin Mullinix

Photographers
Gail Scott Sleeman
Onne Van Der Wal
Skip Brown
Daniel Forster
Steve Mundinger

Inspiration
Simba the Hungry Cat

THE AUTHOR

Julee Roth is a devoted supporter of sailing and sailing instruction. While sailing is a family endeavor, racing is her passion. She owns and races a Lightning and crews aboard many large yachts.

Educated in England, Switzerland and the United States, Julee enjoys living in the mountains. Currently, she spends the winter months in Aspen, Colorado as an instructor with the Aspen Skiing Company. When the snow melts, she spends her summers in Michigan, sailing the Great Lakes.